MYSTIC WAY

(1938)

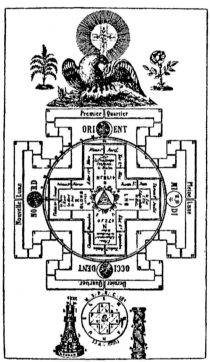

The Philosophical Cross, or Plan of the Third Temple

Raymund Andrea

ISBN 0-7661-0467-2

THE MYSTIC WAY

BY

RAYMUND ANDREA

Author of
" The Technique of the Master," and
" The Technique of the Disciple "

The Modern Mystic's Library
No. 2

London:
KING, LITTLEWOOD & KING LIMITED
SIX BEAR STREET, LEICESTER SQUARE, W.C.2
1938

PRINTED IN GREAT BRITAIN BY THE GARDEN CITY PRESS LTD.
AT LETCHWORTH, HERTFORDSHIRE.

CONTENTS

INTRODUCTION

THE author of this book is known to thousands of students of mysticism. His name is as familiar in the United States, in Denmark, France and even in the Orient as it is in this country. His literary reputation rests upon two important books,—precursors to some extent of the present volume,—*The Technique of the Master*, and *The Technique of the Disciple*, both of which have a ready sale in two continents. The reason for their popularity among students of mysticism is based upon an extraordinary and unique gift, the genius of being able to discourse upon the titles of his books in a manner with which no fault can be found by the most tenacious or dogmatic follower of any particular mystical or occult sect. This in itself is a tremendous achievement. And this result is not obtained by begging any questions, or by artfully skating round debatable points. It is obtained because of an inherent, never-failing instinct for correctly anticipating the requirements of students.

Very few men are equipped psychologically for the exacting task of guiding the neophyte and student through early studies and their attendant, physical, mental and spiritual crises. The mentor of such must possess unusual qualifications. These, Mr. Andrea has in generous measure.

And in addition, the author possesses an excellent literary style. In science, in the arts, and in general literature there are to be found a number of stylists, but since Blavatsky, the literature of the Occult has lacked its artists. Andrea's style is more related to that of Emerson than any other, and it is possible, occasionally, to trace the influence of the American master.

This little book should find favour with two classes of mystics; with those who feel, no matter what their age, either in years or in study, that the face of wisdom is always lovely, and those others who, full of knowledge themselves, have not been vouchsafed the inestimable grace of guiding the uninitiated.

N. V. DAGG.

CHAPTER I

MYSTICAL KNOWLEDGE: ITS PARAMOUNT VALUE

MYSTICISM has been in the world long enough to justify us in regarding it as a fact in world history. It is no longer considered as the crazy belief of a few fanatics of erratic mind and irresponsible action. It is recognised as a branch of knowledge and a way of life. At one time the exclusive study and practice of a privileged circle whose members were scattered here and there in many lands through the centuries, it has come to be a subject of ardent pursuit of students in every grade of society attracted by the higher culture of the present time. Half a century ago books on the subject in the west were comparatively rare, so far as the general public was concerned: to-day, no interested student need want for them. The recondite treatises of the old masters have been resurrected and republished, commentaries on them exist in abundance, and those who have specialised in the subject add their personal testimony to the growing corpus of mystical literature. The mystical renaissance is in full tide.

Paradoxical as it may appear, the church has been one of the first public institutions to recognise this renaissance. We are quick to recognise that which is destined to diminish or supersede our value. That is why the church has recognised mysticism. The institution which, above all others, should have been the very temple of mysticism, the watchful guardian and able exponent of its science and practice, has recognised and—ignored it. Hence the great anomaly of modern times: the mystical church of Christ is abroad in the world; and the house of institutional religion that rejected it, mourns its loss of influence upon the advancing mind which has done for ever with creed and dogma. The evolving mind has always made short work of institutions. The Master Himself did, because He was the supreme mystic. The mystic of to-day dares to follow His example. In olden times he did so, but persecution dogged his footsteps, and he had to hide his light and his knowledge or lose both in an ignominious death. Not so to-day. The ranks are reinforced on every hand. The awakening mind is asserting its freedom and its prerogative, and neither church nor state can dictate to or shackle it. The state, through the instrumentality of its laws, has wisely never attempted to run counter to the free thinking of the subject. The church, on the other hand, sensible that it stands publicly at the bar of intellectual judgment, resents its undignified position and, though fully conscious of its misrepresentation, refuses to make just discrimination and loudly arraigns all and sundry outside its precincts as of irreligious habit.

This much it is necessary to say, if only once more to point the fact that the church has lost its hold upon the modern mind. It is necessary to say it to encourage those who have had the confidence to follow the light of their own aspiring souls and demonstrate the Christ-consciousness fearlessly in their own lives. That is the keynote of the new age. Mysticism looks to no creed, acknowledges no concocted articles of religion, gives no allegiance to church or theologian, ignores the imposing authority of men and priests, and makes humble obeisance to one, and one only, the living, energising spirit within the temple of the soul.

The mystical renaissance dawned in the early years of the present century. It dawned rather suddenly. The Psychic Research Company and the New Thought movement simultaneously let loose across the world a flood of literature which arrested the attention and interest of thinking people everywhere, opening out the possibilities of individual development through application of the thought forces in business and everyday life. Hypnotism and magnetism, healing, magic and personal influence, and many allied subjects, comprised a large section of this literature; and no doubt a good deal of it has been applied to questionable ends. Nevertheless, this literature marked a definite epoch in the evolution of mind. It struck the note of individual mental freedom from bondage to church, school and science, and every other bloated authority. It turned the eyes of the individual upon himself, emphasised his responsibility and his possibility in the scheme of things, and drove home the needed truth that to himself he must look for the evolution of his innate powers and for achievement and success in the world.

A large section of this literature, as said, was devoted specifically to the means and methods of worldly success. That was enough to secure its instant and keen reception; and it has been well employed. But a portion of this literature was of a very different character. It was no less devotedly directed to the possibilities of the spiritual evolution of the individual. Then it was that mysticism began to come into its own. To thousands it meant nothing less than a rebirth in consciousness. Within a few years societies and groups of spiritual culture sprang up on every hand, inaugurated by those who, ahead of the general evolution and aided by Karmic privilege, were already well advanced on the mystic path, and who, through personal teaching or written word, disseminated the ancient truth in acceptable form to thousands of earnest seekers who were literally hungering for true guidance, hitherto lacking, in their spiritual life.

I have a vision of this host of seekers, as they then were: men and women, a large percentage of them, of ripe general culture and high attainments in music, literature and science, who had sounded the depths and shoals of the philosophies of the west and had been repelled by the crude, earthbound findings of glorified science in spite of all its wonders, bored to silence and indifference by the humdrum platitudes of stagnant theologies, all looking towards the far-off horizon and knowing in their hearts there must be a way out and beyond the bounds within which they thought, dreamed and aspired. And countless others standing behind them, not so privileged in culture and achievement, but sound and eager in mind and heart, carrying the same burden of life and hoping for the advent of some new light and leading they knew not whence, to throw a meaning upon life and interpret them to themselves, conscious all the while of a guiding hand toward some unknown goal. Then came the mystical dawn and the whole host moved forward, as if a door of the temple had been open to them, to the portals of which they had been unconsciously led through the years. Upon these seekers a light broke as from another world; it was indeed from another world, on the threshold of which they had been long waiting. None had dared hither to speak of it, in church, college or lecture room. Some knew yet feared to speak: it might have soiled their reputation. I recall a minister of the gospel to whom I gave some of this literature, hoping it might add value to his ministry, and who returned it with the remark that he was too rational and, moreover, all these ideas were in Plato. Perhaps they were, as they were also wrapped up, or enigmatically revealed, in the scriptures of India and Egypt. There they remained for the academicians to juggle with and isolated adepts to demonstrate. Academicians still juggle with them and ecclesiastics expatiate; while from the advancing host of seekers potential adepts are emerging to usher in the new age.

When a new idea arrests and possesses the waiting mind, it is never lost, and the mind moves on. It was so when the idea of the mystical adventure as a way of life entered the field of thought. The waiting had been too long and poignant for the idea to be accepted passively and dismissed. It was seized

upon with inordinate zeal and became at once an
active principle in consciousness and a subject of
profound contemplation. It was placed alongside
philosophy and orthodox belief, investigated deeply
and tenaciously applied, and found to fulfil a human
need where those had signally failed. As for the
intellectualists and the scientists, who had sat so
long in the seat of authority and delivered their
oracles, far from inspired ones, with measured rhetoric to quiescent followers, the advent of the new
idea proved a sore trial to them. They were right
up to a point and within a very limited sphere, and
they have been factors in education. They are
wrong in so far as, a greater idea than they had con-
ceived, with all its potent adjuncts, having cut across
their chosen fields and upset from foundation to
summit, their carefully erected edifice of theory and
discovery, they refuse to acknowledge possibilities
for humanity beyond their own mundane vision.
Moreover, the new idea dealt a sharp blow to the
intellectual pride of these eminent authorities. But,
until that is dissipated—and it is one phase of the
world illusion which has to go before spiritual
liberation is possible—evolution beyond the plane
of mind is at a standstill. So that, holding fast to
their pride of logic and mental acumen, and fearing
a loss of reputation through a change of ground and
countenancing unprofessional innovation, the impersonal and independent seeker is actually a world
ahead of them in theory and in practice.

New ideas impinging upon the public consciousness differ considerably in strength and development. New historical and political ideas, for

instance, are often of tardy acceptance and growth. They enter a field of settled and accepted maxims and experience, and are at once brought to the bar of authority, subjected to examination and jealous scrutiny, and violently opposed it may be for threatening the judgment or adding to the knowledge of those who have said the last word in their respective provinces. Those who are responsible for the innovations know what to expect and are prepared for it. Fierce controversy ensues, but the idea stands there in the full light of day, offspring of a mind that has dared to question the canons of orthodoxy or had the boldness to strike an unexpected blow in the cause of humanity, and there is no getting rid of it. We have seen many instances of this, and it gives us faith in the secret omniscience of man and the intrinsic goodness of his heart. But for the existence of a few bold innovators on this planet, the customs and institutions of men, materialistic philosophies and deadening theologies, even science itself and statutes and common law, would crucify and damn the very soul of man. These innovators do not despise what is ; they recognise the value of what has been; but they will not allow things to remain as they are. They are born enemies of the stagnation which arrests development and prevents amelioration. They are rebels against all that binds, holds and slays the innate power of thought. In former times they paid dearly for their originality and were placed behind bars or sent to the stake. To-day, they startle and raise much opposition; but no sooner have they spoken than they raise a following stronger than the opposition and are respected even when not fully understood. That is because they bring what is needed and awaited. The new idea passes like a beam of light into the public consciousness: there it stays to germinate and grow, and in a shorter or longer time, contingent upon its specific value and energy, opens out a fresh horizon of discovery and hope.

The dawn of the present mystical cycle was analogous to this. The idea was really a very old one, destined to emerge in a new form. It appeared in a shape exactly suited to the exigencies of the people to which it came. The time was propitious, for thousands were waiting for it. In its simplest presentation it voiced the urgent truth that there was a way of life within man which, in a materialistic age, he had entirely overlooked. It stressed the truth that here and now, in the living and suffering heart of a longing humanity, there existed the mystic lamp of the spirit which, with careful nurture, would illumine the dark temple of pain and sorrow, disperse the shadows of perplexity and error, and raise the mortal self into alignment with the divine. It encountered opposition, but of a tempered character, and mainly from the orthodox religionists. They decried it because, they asserted, it turned man from the worship of and reliance upon God and sought to make him self-sufficient and presumptuously his own saviour. A crude argument, and not worth discussion. But the redeeming idea grew apace and struck root in every stratum of society. Even a religious teacher here and there could not resist the appeal and enriching influence of it, and instead of an exponent of the word became an oracle of the spirit. But ecclesiastical law is not abrogated with impunity, and they soon passed away. Having a vital and immortal life, the idea gathered momentum through the years and expanded into a literature of immense range and influence. The east, the home for centuries of mystic lore and practice, aware of the awakening of the west to the science of the soul, gave ample proof of its interest and co-operation in augmenting the literature that taught the mystic way and widening the pathway of mutual understanding between them. Hence it is, that to-day no interested seeker need lack instruction and guidance; for mysticism has placed its indelible insignia upon western thought, openly challenged the strongholds of orthodoxy, and occupies the vanguard of spiritual culture and advancement.

It is claimed that mysticism is a fact in world history. To bring the fact closer to us, let it be said that mysticism is the most important branch of knowledge in the literature of the western world. It is far in advance of the technique of science, for, with all the wealth of discovery to its credit, science relies entirely upon the operation and function of the intellect and the senses for its conquests. It is far in advance of institutional religion, for the latter is directed mainly towards moral culture, which is the refinement and elevation of the emotional life. Theology has nothing to teach it, for it is man's intellectual and formal interpretation of his relationship to God, and of Christ as an historical character who assumes and liquidates in some nebulous way the sins of frail and perishing humanity. Materialistic philosophy is an effort of the reasoning mind to

B

give a logical explanation of the objective world, and is, therefore, a twin brother of theology in its objectiveness. Thus science thrives on the intellect and the senses : theology lives by faith : speculation is the soul of philosophy. Mysticism is spiritual insight and transcends all of them. It unfolds the meaning of man's existence, invests him with a mission in life, places upon him individual responsibility at every step in thought and action, and points the fact that his spiritual redemption is in his own hands and relies absolutely upon the clear recognition of his obligations to himself and his fellow men and in meeting those obligations.

Science consists in the classification of facts and the observation of their correlation, sequence and relative significance, the discovery of laws and self-criticism. Mysticism surpasses the scientific method and occupies itself with the technique of spiritual laws operating in the world and in man. Theology is a system of scientifically critical, historical and psychological patterns and theories, as objective in character as is the science of geology or astronomy. Mysticism passes beyond forms and theories and reveals the inner way of union and communion with the Christ consciousness within man through an experimental ascension of consciousness. Materialistic philosophy is the study of the interconnection of the sciences and their ramifications as part of an organic whole, and the theory of knowledge. Mysticism penetrates to the world of underlying spiritual causes and unfolds the rationale of all knowledge and phenomena. The essential difference between these objective and speculative interpretations and the method of mysticism is summed up in a luminous phrase of the *Mundaka-Upanisad* : " It is not apprehended by the eye, not by speech, not by the other senses, not by devotion or rites ; but he, whose intellect is purified by the light of knowledge, beholds him who is without parts, through meditation."

This simple declaration brings the mind to rest in the basic method of mysticism, that of spiritual meditation which unfolds the inner nature of the soul and evolves that self-knowledge which reveals man as a spiritual entity in a world of silent and potent spiritual forces in which he lives and moves and has his being, to which alone he is responsible and through whose aid alone he can " attain the measure of the stature of the fullness of Christ.

CHAPTER II

MYSTIC MEDITATION

MEDITATION is variously defined as an extension of concentration; a deep, continued reflection upon a religious theme; and, perhaps most aptly, as a process of creation in the silence. The subject abounds in technicalities, if we choose to make it difficult by an elaborate consideration of them. But for the present they are quite unnecessary. I question whether one student in a thousand entering upon this subject is in doubt about the fact or act of meditation, or the value of it, or regards it as a mysterious or exceptional practice. By the time the majority of us reach manhood we have been driven to meditate often and deeply enough to attain any worthy objective, or to get through life at all. Such is my experience; and as I am writing chiefly for the seeker and aspirant, it is my own experience, whatever its value may be, that I propose to consult in an attempt to help him.

I remember that the first teaching I met with on the mystical life was of the simplest character. There were no technicalities and no mystery about it. It pointed the main facts of the mind and the soul; the objective was to educate the former, through a process of alignment, to a recognition of the latter. It advocated the daily visualisation of a quality of character or a condition of life needful to the student, which developed steady concentration of thought upon a specific subject. Thence he passed on in time to brief intervals of suspension of mentation, or pure concentration, an arresting of mind action in order to induce a condition of inward quietude and calmness. Then followed a meditative process, consisting in turning the mind in an unbroken wave upon the realisation of the nature of the soul, which is love. The cumulative results of this practice did as much, and perhaps a good deal more, than the many technical procedures offered by many teachers could have achieved. I derogate nothing from elaborate forms of meditation for specific ends. I know their value; but they belong to an advanced stage of the subject. Here we are clearing the ground for the aspirant for a simple ascent from the everyday, objective consciousness to a more interior condition. That is the object of all meditation. He needs a change of heart to tread the mystic way, and the first steps towards it is a change of mind action. There are many steps, and meditation is a process of ascent, up to the inspirational life of the Christ consciousness, which is the altitude of the mystic way.

The object of meditation is to make conscious contact with the life of the soul. The soul has been designated as an entity which is the offspring of Spirit and Matter, an embodied Son of God, incarnated for the purpose of revealing the quality of the nature of God which is love. Hence will be seen the peculiar value of the above-mentioned meditation as a preliminary technique for releasing the essential nature of the soul. It puts aside all unessentials, all technicalities, all the paraphernalia of theory and speculation, and directs the mind, concentrated and dedicated, forthwith to the realisation of the soul by saturating itself in meditation with that quality at the heart of all, impersonal and illuminating love. In the Bhagavad Gita, the Upanisads, and other sacred books the aspirant is exhorted, but more ceremoniously and with lavish detail and technical references, to constant meditation upon the soul as the mystic way of illumination and freedom from bondage to mental illusion and the domination of the sense life. Realisation of the nature of the soul is the burden of the inspired themes of all these classics.

The aspirant's ascent on the mystic way is a two-fold process of the destruction of form and the building of form, until he enters the life of the soul which is formless. He is imprisoned within the mental and emotional form which his life experience has created: his object is to transcend that form. He is a captive soul within the form which he has with pain, and perhaps all too conscientiously, built for his own use. It is the complex form of personality which battles in the arena of life. If the form is sound, stable and well capacitated, it is fortunate; for then it is a vehicle of studied proportion and efficiency for specific uses and attainments in the world of form in contact with similar types. And in that contact it has its own specific measure of vibration and range of response whereby it acts upon and reacts to other types so functioning. But all advancement, even within the world of form, is made through a series of imperceptible destructions and rebuildings of forms. It is so in the physical and mental life. Constant change is the law. On the ascending arc of physical life a finer and more complicated apparatus of response is constantly replacing one of lower capacity and response, as in the mental life, until age or disease brings the cycle to its close. In the majority this takes place without any speculation into the life of the soul, and the mental and emotional form binds till death. Nor, truly, can the complete dominance of the soul arrest the progress of a life cycle. But it can alter it, unbelievably. The soul can pass beyond the life cycle still captive to the form for a future cycle; or the aspirant can set himself the task of taking the mystic way and, through an ascension of consciousness and vibration and power of repose, transcend the form which holds him prisoner on the mental and emotional level and build a finer form of rarer quality which will afford the soul a way of contact with the threefold personality.

Meditation upon the indwelling soul, the Son of love, is a process of building a form for ascent on the mystic way. We speak of destruction and construction of form. There is something suggestively harsh and drastic in the terms. The impression is unfortunate, but ordinary terms must be used in the endeavour to define and depict subtle inner transformations. But the process of change here is no less indiscernible than in the case of physical and mental processes. It is actually a re-polarisation of consciousness, a directing of the life energy inwards toward the deeper strata of being, instead of upon

the purely mental and objective plane of thought
and action. There is nothing mysterious in this idea
of re-polarisation of consciousness. A little reflect-
tion will convince the aspirant how firmly held he is
within the form of the personal self, of the mind
with its opinions and views, its reasonings, and its
continuous subjection to the influence and agitation
of the sense life, if he recalls those rare moments
which come when the mind is carried beyond itself
into momentary contact with the life of the soul
under the inspiration of the word or action of genius
in the world of literature, music or art. Then it is
that, for a brief moment, soul speaks to soul, recognises its own true nature expressed in others, and
realises its own possibilities. It is a re-polarisation
of consciousness involuntarily made through the
personal form having been suddenly transcended,
its range of response extended, its normal vibrational
measure raised to a larger dimension under the influence of inspirational contact with it of some kind
emanating from a mind functioning from a higher
sphere. It is a foretaste of what the technique of the
mystic way will enable the aspirant to do consciously
for himself at will. It proves conclusively to him
that mind consciousness and soul consciousness are
two distinct organisms, with vastly different values
and possibilities. One functions within and is circumscribed by its self-imposed form: the other is
formless and the source of divine love and of all inspiration. It is the bridging form between the two
which he is to build in meditation, until the form of
the personal self is surmounted and free access to the
soul sphere is made. When, later on the way, the

soul is truly dominant and inspires the whole
personal life, the finer form used to make this contact will be no longer necessary and pass away;
for then there is a constant interplay between
mind and soul, and the afflatus which we ascribe
to genius becomes a normal function of mystic soul
communion.

Hugo expresses very pregnantly this contact with
the soul through meditation. Himself an inspired
writer of remarkable power and seership, this word
picture depicts with singular clarity and truth the
passing beyond the mental form into the soul
through re-polarisation of consciousness, and the
lasting effect registered in the mind through the
process. " Every man has within him his Patmos.
He is free to go, or not to go, out upon that frightful
promontory of thought from which one perceives
the shadow. If he does not, he remains in the
common life, with the common conscience, with the
common virtue, with the common faith, or with
the common doubt; and it is well. For inward peace
it is evidently the best. If he goes out upon those
heights, he is taken captive. The profound waves of
the marvellous have appeared to him. No one views
with impunity that ocean. Henceforth he will be
the thinker, dilated, enlarged, but floating; that is
to say, the dreamer. He will partake of the poet and
of the prophet. Henceforth a certain portion of
him belongs to the shadow. An element of the
boundless enters into his life, into his conscience,
into his virtue, into his philosophy. Having a
different measure from other men, he becomes extraordinary in their eyes. He has duties which they

have not. He lives in a sort of diffused prayer, and, strange indeed, attaches himself to an indeterminate certainty which he calls God. He distinguishes in that twilight enough of the anterior life and enough of the ulterior life to seize these two ends of the dark thread, and with them to bind his soul to life. Who has drunk will drink, who has dreamed will dream. He will not give up that alluring abyss, that sounding of the fathomless, that indifference for the world and for this life, that entrance into the forbidden, that effort to handle the impalpable and to see the invisible; he returns to it, he leans and bends over it, he takes one step forward, then two; and thus it is that one penetrates into the impenetrable, and thus it is one finds the boundless release of infinite meditation."

Every aspirant has, indeed, within him his own Patmos. What his resolve to discover and explore and dwell on it may entail, may be considered hereafter. Here we are considering the form he has to transcend and the form he has to build in order to make the discovery. It is being put to him in the simplest possible way. It can be made, and often is, a very abstruse and complicated matter through the importation of technical formulæ, or by obscuring the issue with symbolical and ritualistic references and observances, all which is perplexing and baffling in the extreme both to the practical student and to the uninitiated. The aspirant has the simple issue before him of electing to remain a prisoner, for a prisoner he is, within the mental and emotional form which experience in the objective world has compelled him to build for his manifold contact and use; or passing beyond the frontier of a circumscribed existence into the mystic realm of the soul which awaits his discovery. His decision in favour of the latter assumes that he accepts the basic truth of mysticism: that he is not a mental being searching for some nebulous and evasive entity known as the soul, but a spiritual entity which is the very centre of all his being, the maintaining, nourishing and energising force, unrecognised though it be, of his mental, emotional and physical life. It is this shifting of viewpoint from the periphery to the centre which inaugurates the building of the new form, the line of communication and transmission, which his meditation is to construct and stabilise and bring into daily use.

An example of the building of form in the mental life may further clarify the subject to the aspirant entering upon the way, and show how the line of communication with the soul is established and vivified so that it becomes a vehicle of transmission of its potencies to the personal life. In this hypothetical case the aspirant has a great love for music and the desire to emulate a great master of it. The master's work is an ideal of transcendent influence to the aspirant and a continuous source of meditation to him. He broods upon it and lives in it daily. It has an attractive force beyond anything else in his life. Whenever his mind is free from occupation with mundane things it automatically reverts to this ideal world of artistic science and expression. So powerful is its influence upon him that his own musical character and execution manifest more and more the form in all its characteristics of the ideal

before him. He veritably builds in mental and
emotional matter a line of communication between
himself and his ideal. He projects himself to and
thinks with and into it. His intense love for it opens
a living way of response whereby his understanding
is broadened, his conceptual powers are enlarged,
his ability to compose and execute is developed, and
his entire musical life enhanced through this process
of sympathetic intercourse between his own world
and that of the master artist.

So it is in building the form in meditation. The
aspirant may take the conception, fundamental to
all his work, of himself as a spiritual entity, the soul
of love at the centre of being, and dwell constantly
in the thought of that essential love nature which he
seeks to express in threefold activity, on the physical,
emotional and mental planes. In so doing he will
be engaged in a method of scientific accuracy and
potency. The soul, which is a ray of the one Impersonal Love, the foundation of human existence,
will respond to recognition. That is the first point
of discovery; the soul awaits recognition by the
mind; it awaits release from the hiddenness and
silence which the established form of personality
imposes upon it. But as soon as the line of communication is open through recognition of and dwelling
in the nature of the soul, a response will take place
in the personal self, and imperceptibly the vibration
of the latter will be heightened and cultured and
take on the tone and colouring of that august influence. Repeated meditation will strengthen the
line of communication, enlarge the channel of transmission, until the mental form has been outgrown

and the note of the soul sounds permanently in the personality.

But is not this relinquishment of the form of personality a surrendering of mental values ? By no means: no more assuredly than the musical aspirant surrenders aught of value in surpassing himself through using the devotional form of access to the master work which is his ideal. Contrariwise, he recognises at every step the reflex action of his devotion and knows himself to be fortified with new ideas and inspiration and becoming a centre of attraction for all that is responsive to his mental note in the world of his art. It is so with the student of meditation dwelling in the mystic and illuminating love of the soul. The influence of that communion is not confined within the personality. It radiates to the four quarters of the earth, and like a powerful light attracts to himself all that is beneficent and uplifting in men and circumstances. All that is surrendered, or automatically passes away from him, is not worth keeping. That which comes to him has an eternal value and raises all he has and is to a new level of life and action. It is a simple truth, but so hard of acceptance for the dominating mind of the west. It is hard to realise how the harmless, compassionate nature of the soul can hold its own against, harder still that it can transcend, the dominant note of the assertive mental life; or, if so, of what use it can be. The aspirant is to put it to the test. Those who have done so can testify to the new values which have come to them.

The finer form is building : the soul responds : the vibration of the personality is heightened : repolarisation of consciousness is gradually taking place. The personality feels the energising and life-giving force of the soul. The influence of the subtle form silently impinges upon other souls and attracts the good in them; more than this, it has an awakening effect upon them. That is one of the most arresting facts observed by the aspirant who follows the mystic way. Those he contacts respond to the note of the life of the soul. This is because he no longer regards them merely as personalities, but as souls in evolution; and that attitude of approach to them calls forth a definite note of response. Nor is this strange, remembering that the soul is the same in all and subject to the same laws of evolution and expression. And intimately associated and at one, as it is, with the unseen hierarchy of Masters and Powers who know its life and watch its onward progress and earnest seizure of opportunity offered it for treading the way to conscious communion with Them, the bridging form not only assures the aspirant of the continuous co-operation of the soul within in all his activities, but brings him more and more within the cognisance of these Higher Powers, who stand ready to assist the process and equip him eventually as a tried and proved aspirant with added senses and faculties for use in some form of world service.

CHAPTER III

THE CONTEMPLATIVE MIND

THROUGH meditation the aspirant makes experimental contact with the nature of the soul. He opens up a direct line of communication between the personality and the spiritual entity which is basic and causal to his threefold expression on the physical, emotional and mental planes of life. Hitherto firmly polarised within this threefold form, he insensibly shifts the polarity of consciousness and lives consciously from a higher and more interior condition, the meeting ground of potent spiritual forces. The habit of meditation increases the sense of reality and purposive influence of the spiritual centre at the heart of life. Even the finer bridging form set up through meditation loses its outline and is finally relinquished as he rests in contemplation upon the life of the soul.

As meditation is an extension of concentration, so contemplation may be considered as intensified meditation. Many text books draw a sharp distinction between meditation and contemplation. In the present connection it is a distinction with very little difference. The simplest definition of meditation is, a serious contemplation of a subject or object;

that of contemplation, meditativeness. Thus they are interchangeable terms. Meditation, again, is defined, in its spiritual application, as a close investigation and analysis of the inward life of its subject or object: contemplation, as a deep and reposeful reception of what that inward life can impart. But we have already defined meditation as a process of making conscious contact with the nature of the soul. In contemplation, it is said, we are not concerned with form, but with the soul or life. Since that is our aim, to know the nature of the soul, contemplation can rightly be considered as an intensified form of meditation.

It is interesting to note that in the famous "Spiritual Exercises" of St. Ignatius, the terms meditation and contemplation are used interchangeably, to the end of an exhaustive exploration and realisation by the exercitant of the subjects set before him. He is given a series of daily contemplations on the Kingdom of Christ and enjoined to meditate along specific lines of thought bearing upon the life and ministry of Christ, all with the object of re-creating and experiencing within himself in the act of devotion the beauty, power and passion of the Ideal Man. This, it will be observed, is somewhat analagous to what the aspirant is to do in building the finer bridging form from the personality to the soul; except that, in the following of the "Spiritual Exercises," the exercitant is bound in his work by churchly and theological beliefs and applications of a personal character, which while they do ennoble the life, yet fail to allow free expression of the soul. Nevertheless, the fact remains that this manual which has been one of the most cherished systems of spiritual discipline in the Roman communion and among those of the monastic life for centuries, enjoins in its contemplations that the exercitant meditate point by point upon the historical events of the life of the Master as outlined in the scripture, until the meaning and emotional content of those events become living and present to the mind and heart of the meditator. "He is told to ask himself: 'Who is Christ? Why does He do this? Why does He avoid that? What do His commands and example suppose or suggest?' In other words, he is made to do some deep personal thinking, perhaps for the first time in his life at least on such serious subjects. Inevitably his thoughts will be introspective and he will inquire why the patience, the humility, the meekness, the obedience and other virtues, which are so vivid in the personality of the Ideal Man, are so weak or perhaps non-existent in his own soul. The scrutiny of the conscience, which is nothing but self-knowledge, is one of the principal exercises, for it helps us to discover what perhaps never before struck us, namely that deep down in our natures there are tendencies, inclinations, likes, dislikes, affections, passions which most commonly are the controlling and deciding forces of nearly all our acts; and that some of these tendencies or inclinations help, while others hinder, growth in virtue. Those that do not help, but on the contrary impede or prevent, our spiritual progress are called by St. Ignatius inordinate affections, that is tendencies, which are out of order, which do not go straight for the completeness

C

and perfection of a man's character, but on the contrary, lead in the opposite direction. The well-balanced mind will fight against such tendencies, so as to be able to form its judgments and decide on its course of action both in the major and minor things of life without being moved by the pressure or strain or weight of the passions. It will look at facts in the cold light of reason and revealed truth, and will then bend every energy to carry out its purpose of spiritual advancement."

I have not quoted the above authority with the object of advocating the " Spiritual Exercises " as a suitable method for the aspirant on the path, but as an example of the logical and searching technique the exercitant employs in his contemplative life. Their unsuitability for the aspirant lies also in the fact that the procedure adopted is morbidly intro-spective and fastens the attention continuously and minutely upon the imperfections of mind and heart; and instead of stabilising consciousness in the soul, tends to confine it within the threefold form from which it is the intention of the aspirant to free him-self. For while it is true that the contemplative life is hindered by the imperfections of the moral nature, the moral virtues do not belong to the contempla-tive life essentially, since the end of the contempla-tive life is the consideration of truth. The contem-plative life has one act, which is the contemplation of truth. And it is to be remembered that the aspirant does not pass from the meditative term, during which he is building the finer form for entering into the nature of the soul, to the contemplative life in a single bound. During that term, while repolarisation of consciousness is gradually taking place, there is a life to be lived and much to be done of no mean depth and quality. It is then he is building in the moral virtues, the essential mystic qualities, upon which the contemplative life may securely rest. It is not to be expected that the threefold personal life which he brings to the task is fashioned ready to his hand to meet the exigencies of that keen vibration without discipline. It never is, no matter what the intellectual status or moral equipment of the aspirant may be. In fact, the more efficient and stable these factors are, the greater often is the necessity for breaking down the established form which is normal to both. Heretical and unpardonable as it may appear, the notoriously good man may have the most to do here. Has it ever occurred to the aspirant how a virtue can hinder and blind him? He will realise it on the mystic way as nowhere else. Introspection has its uses and can teach him something: it can also lead him to place such an emphasis upon his virtues as to overlook, not his vices, but his own selfishness. His meditative term will teach him that the love of the soul is beyond virtue and non-virtue; that it is compassion in action, and calls for a new standard of values, and a different code of ethics.

The aspirant will appreciate this beautiful mystical note: " The contemplative mind tramples on all cares and longs to gaze on the face of its Creator." It is also written that, " in gazing, or even attempting to gaze, on the ineffable mystery of his own higher nature, he himself causes the initial trial to fall on him." The trial is precipitated through the influence of the soul impinging more and more

strongly upon the personal life. The aspirant has
passed beyond the form of the latter and now recognises its limitations. He stands a little in advance
of his former self and becomes a critic of that self.
That is a trial, for there is nothing so disconcerting
as coming to a realisation of ourselves. Sometimes
a student is so annoyingly humiliated at what the
first attempt to gaze upon the reality of himself dis-
closes, that nothing will induce him to go further,
and he finishes with the good work then and there.
He cannot bear to look upon his own weakness: his
strength is all; and he retreats to the form where he is
safe and undisturbed, until some happy catastrophe
of life helps to break the illusion for him. In a case
of this nature, the aspirant has usually entered upon
the quest out of curiosity, or under persuasion of
others, without a certain preparedness of mind
which is willing to pay the price of advancement and
knowledge. But it argues a poor pupil anywhere in
life who is not prepared to accept the discomforts
incident to readjustment which a necessary discipline
entails. It is a curious trait in human nature, that a
student devoted to an art or science will work and
deny himself and suffer any privation to reach excel-
lence in it, that his personal life may be enriched and
shine with a borrowed lustre, yet will question the
value or retreat from a more interior discipline which
will lead him to the very fount of inspiration and
genius within him. For nothing less than this is the
aim and end of the contemplative life. But it has its
own price and exacts a discipline no less crucial and
painstaking, yet far more subtle and reactive, than
that demanded for any intellectual acquisition. An

aspirant does not usually go this way with whole-hearted intent, and rarely passes into true contemplation, until he has come to the end of his mental resources. Consider the fact. A peculiar strength is required and must have generated in the personality before a man is ready to seek the peace and rest, and bear the force, tension and inspiring domination of the soul. " The contemplative life is sweetness exceedingly lovable." That sounds very antithetical to the active life demanded of the practical mystic. But note this : " Those who wish to hold the fortress of contemplation, must first of all train in the camp of action." That is the complementary note. It is the keen life of action which fits the aspirant to pay the price of discipline which enables him to hold the fortress of contemplation. And it is just because some aspirants start away with high hopes from dabbling in the mysterious and magical without any sound moral and mental background to lean upon, and attempt to storm the holy precincts of the soul without due preparation, that they are thrown back as by unseen and violent hands upon their own unpreparedness and taught that they cannot invoke the sacred guardian of their own immortal self with impunity.

In building the finer form through meditation for access to the soul, the guardian of the entrance is invoked. The voice of conscience sounds in the personal life with startling emphasis. It indicates a new standard of values which are at cross purposes with life within the threefold form he seeks to transcend. Meditation sounds the chord of dissonance 'between the two. The contemplative life is to

resolve that chord into one of harmonious attune-
ment. The soul has a vibration, a tempo, out of
proportion to that of the personality. The two
cannot become one, or we should be translated
beyond any further contact with mundane things.
But the contemplative life demands an approximation, a re-orientation of the personal life, a degree of
fineness and spiritual culture, a basic and vibrant
goodness of heart and mind, to bear and use sanely
and unselfishly the powerful vibration of the soul.
Where this is not the case there is danger, because
the meditative form invites the energy of the soul
into the personality; and if the latter does not,
through the force of aspiration, right interpretation
and proper adjustment, raise and employ its life
and faculties on the terms and after the law of that
down-pouring and quickening energy, the increased
stimulation will accentuate the mental and emotional
expression in undesirable ways within the old form.
Then we have an instance of an aspirant, engaged
upon the mystical novitiate, but giving the un-
pleasant impression of a person overwrought, out of
control, erratic, proud and egotistic, autocratic and
domineering, with all the elements of an unprepared
and uncultured personality life urged to expression
in their worst form. That is why physical age and
world experience play a far more important part
in the preparation for the mystic way than many
think. I have known aspirants in their third decade
lament the fact that they have not grasped and been
able to apply the technique of the higher stages of
the way. It has been well for them: they had
neither the judgment, breadth of understanding,

not the common sense to apply what they already knew. They were building the meditative form, the soul was transmitting its impressions to the mind, but the brain lacked the strength and flexibility, which only varied activity and experience could give, to interpret and apply correctly what was imparted.

The history of practically all mystics of note reveals that they have been individuals of strong character and ample experience, who have sounded the depths of life and reached a constitutional matureness. Yet it is often thought that these are chosen souls whom God has kept apart and sheltered from the common way of life for a special work. That they were destined for special work may be true: it is not true that they were saved from deep immersion in common life experience. They were pre-eminently those who had been thrust into the furnace of life and made to suffer the keenest. That is why, when the fire had done its work in them, the light of the love of the soul shone through them so radiantly. They laid their lives upon the altar with both hands and the purifying fire separated the gold from the dross with all intensity and purpose. Let the aspirant ponder on that. I ask him whether it has ever occurred to him that his virtues can hinder and blind him ? Well, when he comes to his meditative form he brings all his set virtues and principles with him, the standard of his mental and emotional life : but the soul has a different set of values. They do not discountenance his moral standard or oppose his mental integrity ; but they show how these can limit him. It is not difficult to see why this should be. The form of personality is a self-erected structure of being and doing in accordance with a relative standard of correctitude and expression; a structure of opinion, belief and living built up mainly from family, religious, professional or other human contacts, and conforming to an accepted ritual of respectability and good report. The soul is formless, knows nothing of respectability or conformity, and heaves opinions, beliefs and formalities headlong. The mystical scripture says that the disciple must renounce the idea of individual rights and the pleasant consciousness of self-respect and virtue. Now, this is a profound truth which the contemplative life will prove to the aspirant. It will so upset the narrow platform of his formal life, that if he has not brought with him the well-tried strength of large experience and the high resolve of spiritual adventure, he will believe he is losing his soul instead of finding it. Think how we are hedged in by what we believe, what we are, what others think we should be; how we watch our good name and reputation because others have given them to us, with what animal ferocity we fight to score a point, to what lengths we go to win a little prestige, and withal, the pride we have in our self-righteousness which keeps us a world apart from a soul towering far above us. The love of the soul which the contemplative life awakens is a flaming sword which destroys all this. If aught of this lives within the form when the awakening comes, it will have to go.

The meditative form opens the way to this; and during the building of it the aspirant will have ample time to study the direction in which it is leading him. It is not a swift and spectacular process. The personality form is not one that surrenders easily its life and character ; therefore there will be ample time to count the cost before he is called upon to pay it. Nevertheless the law is, that what he seriously meditates upon and contemplatively dwells in, will react upon him proportionably to the intentness of his effort. If he evokes the soul, the influence of the superphysical world in which it inheres will impress and seek to dominate the personality, and the degree in which the latter is out of alignment, whether in the assertion of virtue or non-virtue, will determine the extent and rigour of the task of surmounting the form which hinders him.

There are then three major steps which lead the aspirant on from the personal to the impersonal, from the form life of the personality to the formless life of the soul, from consciousness stabilised and confined within the mental and emotional selfhood to a translated, a repolarised consciousness impregnated and inspired by the life of the soul. Concentration enables him to focus the thought forces with intentness and purpose : meditation builds the finer form and opens a line of communication between mind and soul : emergence of the love force of the soul as a consequence induces the attitude of contemplation in the aspiring consciousness, which seeks to transcend the limits of form. The same stages are also mystically interpreted respectively as, cogitation, meditation and contemplation. Cogitation comprises perceptions of the senses in taking cognizance of effects, visualisations of the imagination,

and the reason's discussion of that which conduces
to the truth in view; in a word it is any actual
operation of the intellect, and has been pertinently
called "the mind's glance which is prone to wander."
Meditation is "the survey of the mind while occu-
pied in searching for the truth." Contemplation
is the simple act of gazing on the truth; "the soul's
clear and free dwelling upon the object of its gaze."
It is the second stage which begins to try out the
aspirant and determines his fitness for the mystic
way. It is the stage when the soul, mind and brain
are being brought into alignment. The mind responds to the soul's vibration, which quickens its
own through the downflow of force and impressions
of a larger and spiritual life; and the brain, accustomed to a settled mode of response and action, has
much to overcome. If the mind can accept the truth
released from the soul, a flexible brain will soon fall
into line and become the obedient instrument for
the expression of it. But this is rarely the case,
except in those of very mature inward growth.
Much of the difficulty of the way lies just there,
when the powerful life of the soul is drawing the
mind consciousness upward from its accustomed
seat of cognition and operation to a higher and inclusive vision of men and circumstances. It is just
there that the cry of loneliness and separation and
misunderstanding arises in the history of those who
have become contemplative. They perforce had to
leave so much behind which at the time seemed so
very precious to them; much which they would
have retained if they could, because it had been a
source of legitimate pleasure and comfort and had

fostered harmonious relationships in their environment; much that was orthodox and good in its place and which gave them a reputation for judgment and worldly sense and easy good fellowship with others. But the values of the soul do not lie in these things. They emanate from the law of the soul which is indifferent to relative goodness, relationships and personal reputation. These are, admittedly, hard sayings. But the inspiring inflow of the impersonal and inclusive love of the soul alters all things. It brings new ideas which antagonise the old, different ideals which prompt to new fields of endeavour, a spiritual knowledge which tests old friendships severely and often leads to estrangement. It alienates sympathies which the ties of years have made dear to us. It reveals weakness where we thought we were strongest. The stable balance of the whole life within form is disturbed and has to strike a new poise. All this the contemplative mind brings upon itself through the force of its own aspiration. It is the inevitable accompaniment of the release from form and passing into the life of the soul. And if the aspiration is strong and the will resolved, nothing else matters; neither pain, nor loss, nor disappointment, ridicule or any other obstacle or hindrance, will deflect the aspirant's firm step and progress on the mystic way.

CHAPTER IV

MYSTIC INSPIRATION

WHEN we know that "the contemplative life is sweetness exceedingly lovable," we have experimental knowledge of the nature of the soul. It is a condition of quiet enjoyment of spiritual love and peace, wherein the voice of personality is silenced and the life of form transcended. It may also suggest a condition so alien and remote from modern existence as to be regarded askance by all but a few of privileged development, and circumstances. Yet such is the condition, and the mystic way invites to it. It is regarded askance by the majority because they are so immersed within the life of form— necessarily and unavoidably in the circumstances it may be, but that is not the point—and can only think and act in accordance with the rhythm established therein, that consequently any idea of a larger rhythm beyond form which is grounded upon love and repose and finds its greatest power in quiet self-containment, is to them either a negation of life or a renunciation of its most important values. Nor can a different attitude be expected in them until those values lose their compulsive attraction through failing them at critical junctures of life and

44

they turn with wise reflection to consider the one
stable factor of existence, the soul and the meaning
and purpose of its incarnation.

"Meantime within man," said Emerson, "is the
soul of the whole; the wise silence; the universal
beauty, to which every part and particle is equally
related; the eternal One." In that realisation the
"sweetness exceedingly lovable" is touched, im-
pregnates the aspirant, in mystic contemplation.
Thence may arise mystic inspiration. The term
usually denotes the action of the creative impulse
as manifested in high artistic achievement; but in
its present application it might be more particularly
denoted as the divine afflatus. It is this peculiar,
distinctive and urgent influence of the soul which
comes to fruition in special instances in the contemplative state on the mystic way. Not a little curiosity
and speculation are awakened in those who observe
the results of this superphysical contact in an initiate
of mysticism. But he who has it is usually at a loss
to define it. Why? Not only because the spontaneous expression of the soul defies adequate
definition, but because, unless soul speaks to soul,
misunderstanding is inevitable. If we asked a great
artist how he produced the grand effects he does with
such magical ease and sureness and the absence of
all apparent effort, he would be unable to give us the
formula. There is no formula. He could point
undoubtedly to unremitting labour and crucifying
attention to detailed procedure in the past; but that
is only the way of preparation, as is the technique
of the mystic way for the aspirant who now expresses with abandon the life of the soul. In both

cases the same agency is at work. The vehicles of expression are prepared through endless toil for the purpose in view ; then the form of preparation is surpassed and the inspiration of the soul dominates the artist's work, as the mystic afflatus descends upon the dedicated aspirant and prompts him to being and doing better than he knows. From that complete surrender of himself to the life of God within him, from the silence in which he lives when the personal self has lost character and voice, comes the infallible guidance and moving influence of the divine monitor which touches with its genius the work of his hands.

This divine creativeness is the highest function of the soul. There are many states and graces of the mystical life, each of individual value and beauty in its own domain and bearing witness to the awakening and supremacy of the soul in man ; but it is submitted that there is none that surpasses in divinity and worth the creative attribute which instils into the contemplative mind representative types of divine wisdom for the enlightenment and inspiration of humanity. But there is need for careful discrimination in this matter on the part of the aspirant. It is true that ardent natures often go farthest ; they also pay sharp penalties for their enthusiasm. Some aspirants are so possessed with their own sense of efficiency when once they take the mystic way, that they lose both the judgment and the discrimination customary to them in ordinary life and make the most extravagant claims of an inspirational character. It cannot be too often affirmed that if the creative life of the soul is to find expression through the aspirant and be of real service in the world, it must have a well ordered mind at its disposal. Nevertheless, the belief is common, even when thinking of the Masters of the path, that the latter because of some special privilege or evolution demonstrate their technical brilliancy through an act of grace ; that so ordinary a function as the intellect in the exercise of its various faculties is not in requisition and, indeed, is not necessary ; that by supernal prerogative they exercise their multifarious abilities spontaneously and with scant reliance upon the vehicles of expression on which we have to rely. Nothing could be further from the truth. Should the aspirant reach a stage of pupilage under a Master, he will receive one of the most impressive lessons the mystic way can teach him. He will witness a demonstration in the intricacies of personality technique as applied to the threefold life which will astound him. Not only in the direction of spiritual exaltation, insight and prescience, but in the knowledge and exercise of faculties and powers in the purely mental realm he will see an example of developed and organised forces which might well thoroughly dishearten him, but that the fact of witness to it is a promise of tuition to like mastery. That demonstration of Master inspiration is a dialectic of the soul ; but it is based upon the logic of an organised mind. The latter must come first. There must be an architectural order and symmetry in the mental life, a logicalness and depth, precision and clear-sightedness, which are proof against illusion and glamour, if the truth of the soul is to be correctly recorded and transmitted in a form for human helpfulness. For under the accelerated vibration to which the aspirant is now subjected, if the substructure of the mental life is not deep and strong, balanced and formal—we cannot do without form ; we but transcend it to return and use it from a higher level of insight and power—the most inconsequential phenomena may haply be considered as of momentous value. It often is so. Hence we see among aspirants of indifferent preparation many instances of sentimental and incoherent outpourings of sub-conscious accumulations into a passive and ill-regulated mind which are believed to be nothing less than divine revelations. The history of spiritualism affords many examples of this : and so does that of pseudo-mysticism. I have had the privilege of reading some of these revelations, still awaiting publication, and no greater travesty of authentic mystic inspiration could well be imagined. True mysticism dissociates itself absolutely from these scripts of automatic delivery from dark and doubtful sources.

Mystic inspiration is the voice of spiritual intensity and truth, of the soul itself in moments of high exaltation, and its utterance bears the stamp of originality and certitude. It does not derive from a condition of passivity, but from an altitude of positive receptiveness, in which the whole living organism is at high tension at a point of maturity of development in all its functions. It is, if one dare say it, a reflex action of the inner fire following upon a prepared assault upon the Kingdom of God within, and endows the aspirant with the ability to translate the divine types into language and action in world service. Note the implications of this fact. Lesser things than this may come on the way, but they are only the alphabetical articulations of the language of fire. It is pardonable if these intimations are mistaken by the aspirant for the afflatus itself. It is something to enter into the first fruits of the life contemplative, and there is no wish to disparage them. But they are little better in value than the high moments of the intellect in its best state. They are still within the life of form. He seeks the divine creativeness which emanates from the fire of the resident soul, dominant and active in its own form-less realm. Comparatively few attain it because the term of discipline is long and exacts much. Therefore many are tempted to take the easier path of passive surrender and mediumship and rest content with the reflex communications of other minds no further evolved, perhaps a good deal less, than their own. Yet this is less than a caricature of mystic inspiration and never made an aspirant a teacher of men.

It is obvious that during the endeavour to enter upon the contemplative stage there will ensue certain reactions to the extension of consciousness achieved, and the awakening of the soul will announce itself in different ways according to the type of aspirant. Hence in some, emotional stresses are in evidence and voices or visions are concomitants. These phenomena are common among aspirants. Whether the voices come from without or within and what is the precise interpretation of that which is sensed, are usually matters of speculation; and in the case of visions of various kinds, such as lights

D

and colours, geometrical figures and fugitive forms, these are unconnected apparently with anything in the objective life of the individual and become a common source of perplexity through the absence of any logical relationship or interpretation. In others, such phenomena as telepathy, psychometry and automatic writing are experienced ; and whereas the two former are open to reasonable explanation and capable of test as to accuracy of results obtained, the latter is usually a symptom of mediumship which calls for positive mental interposition to offset it. The gift of tongues and the grace of prophecy have, in common with the above, been considered as of secondary importance and of little objective value ; signs of morbid disorder and neuropathy and therefore rejected by true mysticism. But this assertion is open to objection. They may be classed as inferior gifts to, and possibly hindrances in the way of, that condition of mystical realisation wherein all objective life is transcended and forgotten and the mystic dwells in bliss and peace in the radiance of the soul. Those are rare moments of the super-life when the highest things we know or can conceive are not worth the having. If they come, it is well ; but if they incline the aspirant to discountenance the instrumentalities of active service in the world, it is not well they should be frequent. The gift of tongues and the grace of prophecy are indeed possible emergencies of the mystic inspiration of the soul ; so much so, that they are rarer than true inspiration itself and would probably only emerge for the purposes of special service.

Putting aside therefore both the phenomenal aspects of the mystical pilgrimage, and the exceptional gift of tongues and the grace of prophecy, let us consider the basic fact of inspiration, to which the former may be stepping stones and of which the latter may be emergencies for extraordinary service. Some authorities assert that the inspirational condition on the mystic way is of comparatively rare attainment, and the majority of genuine aspirants only reach the phenomenal stages mentioned, or at most the condition of ecstasy. I do not think this statement is open to question. Those with experience of various classes of aspirants on the path would probably confirm it. I offer two factors for consideration in support of it. One is, that special and congenial circumstances are requisite in which daily preparation can be followed in order to invite the mystic afflatus. This does not imply what is called retirement from the world, so much as certain favourable surrounding conditions which are peculiarly helpful in isolating the aura and rendering it non-conductive of disturbing vibrations from the world of form. If this is questioned, let it be remembered how much positive cancellation of intruding elements is necessary during the meditative term in order to attain the quietude and non-resistance in which alone the contemplative state can bear fruit in the life. But of far greater importance than this is the second factor; so much more important that it can considerably minimise the factor of circumstances and render it almost negligible. I refer to the degree of inward evolution of the aspirant. Indeed we touch very closely here the secret of mystic inspiration.

Let us consider two types of aspirant. One is taking methodically the necessary stages of the way, and every step is hard won ground. It is new ground : he brings no reserve of development with him. It is his first speculation into the life of the soul, and even years of study and meditation directed to development have only just succeeded in changing somewhat the established rhythm of the personality and enabled him to recognise some response from the soul as an active force in his life. Certain phenomenal aspects of this development may be vouchsafed him and are an indication that one or other of the psychic centres is functioning. Beyond that stage of mystical gift or grace he may not proceed far in the present cycle. There is a constitutional accommodation to be made to give reliable effect to that new aspect of consciousness. He cannot pile phenomena on phenomena at a rapid pace. Fortunately this is so, for mental equilibrium and physical health are of first importance ; and to force development at the expense of these is not the aim of a wise aspirant. And if this phenomenal stage has been reached for the first time in the course of his evolution, it is obvious, bearing in mind the slow processes of nature in consolidating a new condition of extraordinary functioning in the constitution that he will not supersede this condition very quickly and in one life. Nor do I think he would be anxious to do so ; for the opening up of psychic avenues of contact and information will prove all too engrossing and demand all the ability of adjustment he can bring to it : and it is certainly better that he should endeavour to thoroughly understand and accommodate the personal life to that which is given, putting it to such legitimate uses as he can to enhance his technical grasp of the psychic intricacies of his nature as they emerge. Therefore, in such a type as this, and authentic data show that the majority of students fall within this category, it may well be doubted whether the flowering of the mystical life, which confers superior graces and among them possibly the special creative function of inspiration, will be attained in the present cycle.

In contrast with this is the rarer type, but of which there are a few examples to-day, as there have been many formerly. It is that of the aspirant who takes the mystic way with a burden of past knowledge and development to his credit, and who has passed through the preliminary stages in a former cycle. Avoiding technicalities, it may be briefly said that his psychic nature is well developed, that the heart and head centres are aligned and functioning; in which case, the phenomenal aspects will be either rapidly revived and retraced, or transcended completely without conscious memory and review, and the higher life of the soul will be brought quickly into requisition. Then we may have the inspired teacher or doer, expressing the divine types of wisdom in some form of artistic comment or practical action in world service. But by no means always. It does not follow that, because of this maturity of development and swift alignment with the life of the soul, the mystic afflatus should necessarily become part of the aspirant's equipment. In my opinion, true mystic inspiration is only likely to appear in conjunction with mature inner development and for a very special purpose, as in some form of leadership or literary expression. But the higher stages of the way confer a diversity of gifts, and that which is given will be suitable to the type of recipient and that which he can best use. I have known many recipients of mystical gifts, but rarely one who could claim the surpassing gift of inspiration. Yet these aspirants have been of marked inner development and in a notable stage of pupilage. Practically all of them were contemplatives and manifested one or other mystical gift or grace, yet none showed the special gift of inspired utterance.

What does this fact reveal? Why is it that even among those who have been long on the way, have entered into the life of the soul and, moreover, received extraordinary graces and the gifts of lucidity, vision and divine love, there is wanting that climaxing gift of the inspired word which burns into the souls of men with irresistible force and persuasiveness and thereby proves its validity? It is because the personal life has not yet surrendered itself so completely to the compulsive fire of the informing soul as to forget its formal utterance and demand with utmost urgency that the voice of living truth within the veil shall take its place. If the aspirant would have an example of the mystic afflatus using a prepared and sanctified personality for the blessing of man, he would do well to peruse the " Imitation of Christ." It is a classic example of the contemplative mind at the highest point of exaltation, wherein the fire of mystic inspiration has taken complete possession of its instrument and expressed through it a theme of commanding exhortation and instruction. Lofty and beautiful in conception, yet simple in diction, the compressed fervour of its spiritual cadence moves and incites heart and mind as do the words of Christ Himself. Let the aspirant ponder deeply upon the fourth chapter: " Of the king's high way of the holy cross " in that book, and note how, in its brief, inclusive and pious comment, it surveys and enunciates with inspired vision the mystic way of ascension to union and communion with Christ as by a divine fiat. What does *this* fact reveal? That the disciple became as his Master and uttered the wisdom of His presence. Therein lies the secret of the mystic afflatus. That is why it is rarely encountered, even among those on the mystic way. What is lacking is the simplicity, the self-abandonment and the divine passion of the soul resurrected from the dark tomb of selfhood, consequent upon the realisation in the heart of the heavy burden which lies even now upon the heart of Christ in humanity. Until that realisation comes the aspirant may be contemplative and dwell in " the sweetness exceedingly lovable," but the fire of the hidden temple will not become articulate in gracious utterance to enlighten and bless those who stand without.

CHAPTER V

THE AWAKENING FIRE

MUCH has been written, and a good deal indiscriminately, about the spiritual fire and its awakening in students on the path, as a means of attainment of supernormal powers and insight into supersensible life. Some writers refer to it briefly and with a note of warning, marking strongly the ill effects which are likely to follow any forced attempts to arouse the fire. Other writers give, without discrimination or note of caution, experimental instruction of various kinds for the specific purpose of bringing the fire into action through the agency of the psychic centres in the body and brain, with large promise of the highest rewards of development and demonstration if consistently followed. The yoga systems of the east, now widely disseminated in the west, refer to this attainment as a matter of course and are prolific in methods relating to the awakening of the fire. Indeed, they aver that the awakening is the first major step on the way for the demonstration of the singular powers with which the yogi is credited.

In that matter of the awakening fire, in which so many are interested, students fall mainly into two classes : those who confine themselves to sane and safe methods of study and meditation hoping that in good time when they are inwardly fitted for it, they will receive adept instruction in the actual process of awakening; and those who promptly seize upon any available methods which promise success and exploit them to the limit for good or ill, intent as they may be on high attainment. I do not propose to instruct the one class, or to be a critic of the other.

The technique of the inner life affords no sharp demarcation between the mystical and the occult aspects of experience. Occultism and mysticism each has its own literature, and there are certain differences between the methods they suggest: the former often emphasises, with a hint of superiority, that it is the way of the head; while the latter, equally conscious of a gracious elevation, reminds us that it is the way of the heart. As a matter of fact, the rightly balanced and fully developed aspirant blends both in a fine equipoise and demonstrates the powers and graces of both in harmonious conjunction. It is well to remember that the Masters of the present cycle demand equally in their pupils the love and compassion of the heart and the organised mind and will, to carry out efficiently their work. And if, in the aspirant, either the mystical or the occult aspect is overdeveloped at the expense of the other, the immediate objective of his training will be a balanced and co-ordinated expression of both. There are phases of inner culture and experience and reactions which are common to both. The name we give them matters little: the aspirant on the way is our concern. If the mystic, in high emotional stress, disparages the logical thought structure of the occultist as professionalism, the need of the mystic is not far to seek. If the occultist, secure in his hard won knowledge, forgets that love must yet add fire to all his thought, the time is not far distant when the heart will rise through suffering to claim its own. There is a middle path, and it is that of the new age, which demands an equal development of the life of the heart and of the head ; and though I write of the mystic way, there is no intention of giving to the term the limited application it has in the minds of many aspirants, which is that of undisturbed personal enjoyment of the secret heritage of the soul, with faint purpose to give it concrete and masterful expression in some form of service to the world.

I begin with this basic article of belief, and affirm that the aspirant who is consciously using the technique of the way within himself and in world service, is unconsciously awakening the spiritual fire and is subject to its influence in thought, speech and action. I further affirm that the technique, in its true form, is only to be found in those in whom some aspect of the fire is awakened and in action. There may appear to be exceptions to this ; but in those cases in which the fire is prematurely awakened through methods of personal experiment, thus forcing them ahead of the normal evolution of the way, we shall probably find that the technique, as I have outlined it, has no place in the life, or is considered as of secondary importance. This may be for good or ill, contingent upon the health and balance and the objective of the experimenter. The objective in such cases is usually one of phenomenal demonstration,

and this can admittedly take place without any reference whatever to technical achievement in the service of the Master.

I am not concerned here with these cases in which
forced methods have brought the fire into operation
for purposes of phenomenal demonstration. I believe that some danger attends indiscriminate development. I have no doubt that some individuals of
sound constitution and mental equipment have made
considerable progress in this way; while others,
of indifferent health and unstable mentality, yet believing all things possible, have proved to be
totally unequal to the strain imposed upon body and
brain, and the reactions have been serious and re-
sulted in wrecked lives.

In the case of the aspirant who is using the
technique of the Master, a condition of far different
import and value comes under consideration. All
is normal here; that is, however abnormal his
development and experience may appear from the
average standpoint, they are consistent with the
normal treading of the way. In discussing the conditions of the technique I mentioned that the
possession of it reveals a very special development
which brings the aspirant into close co-operation
with the Master in his work. He is then no longer
an aspirant, but a disciple of the mystic way, aware
of his status upon it and consciously using the
technique in some kind of world service; in which
case, he will be constantly passing into new experience of the ways and means of its application and
making very important discoveries within himself as
he pursues his appointed task.

What relation exists between the technique and the awakening fire ? How does the operation of the technique lead to its awakening ? What ground is there for affirming that the fire is in process of evolution in the disciple ?

The relation between the technique and the fire is a subtle and intricate one. It is no less real, but as difficult to define, as is the magnetic quality which the great artist infuses into the execution of a master-piece. This quality is a part of the latter's technical equipment. They develop simultaneously and cannot be separated. If we could eliminate the magnetic quality of his work he would cease to be a master artist although he may still rank as a musician. If the fire is inactive in the disciple, he may be a disciple still, but not a technician of the way in the sense in which I use the term. As there are many grades of musical executants below that of the supreme artist of magnetic quality in execution, so there are many grades of mystical discipleship ; but he whose technical expression bears testimony to the awakening fire within him belongs to a distinct and advanced grade.

Now, this magnetic quality in the artist's execution is of the nature of the very fire of the soul. It expresses itself in a rare combination of elements which we recognise as tone, magical in its beauty, depth and pathos, religious in its intensity and influence, simplicity, strength and naturalness, which carry us in spirit to the fount of creation itself. In like manner, the spiritual fire, stirred to action in the disciple's constitution through the long prayer of devoted service to his fellowmen and the giving of

his life in self-abnegation that thereby some might
be raised to hope and conquest in a perplexing and
suffering world, comes to stamp upon his life expression the fine nuances of spiritual sensitivity and
creativeness which enable him to reflect the tone
and pathos, the simplicity, strength and naturalness,
the speaking interludes and divine silences of the
presence of the Master. His thought is original in
conception, swift, sure and dynamic in force and
direction ; his speech, penetrating, concise and
illuminative, carries the intonations of the mystic
art of the soul ; his action, considered, mature and
inspired, is born of compassion and harmlessness.
If this is not so, it is not the ideal that is out of drawing ; the flower of the technique has not opened in
the soul. We are dwelling upon the fragrance of
that blossom which the suffering and experience of
long probation has produced. This fragrance is the
fiery quality in the technical equipment of the disciple, as the magnetic quality pervades and imparts
illustrious character to the technique of the artist.
In both instances, the soul has awakened within
itself the chord of the essential harmony which is
the fire of the divine life. It is difficult to define, and
is so evasive of analysis except through the merest
hints, as to be recognised only by those who stand
near the precincts of its own secret domain.

How does the operation of the technique conduce
to this awakening ? The work of the advanced soul
in evolution establishes a claim upon super-nature,
and under the law of compensation that claim is met.
There may be no consciousness of claim, or reward,
but the law recognises the claim and there is reward.

The technique works from out the realm of super-
nature, and in the interest of its own efficiency it fur-
nishes a basis of power and inspiration which ensures
the advancement of itself. The mind, brain and ner-
vous systems cannot of themselves give these. They
are the instruments of inspiration, not the inspiring
agent. They must be fortified by the fiery essence of
the indwelling spiritual self. And the daily consecrated use of these instruments of the self in the work
of raising and inspiring human life spontaneously
releases this essence, until every aspect of their
activity responds to the quickened vibration of
this superior energy. If it is said that it is a matter
of vibrational impulses acting upon the prepared
vehicles of the disciple, we shall avoid the bewilder-
ing technical terms of the textbooks which, scientific
in treatment as they are, yet make the subjects
abstruse and difficult of personal application. A
simple illustration will suffice. Continuous physical
or mental application to an exercise or study opens
up a channel of invitation to new energy and thought
leading to increased ability in either direction. The
greater the use the larger the response. There is a
demand upon energy and thought to meet the need
of quickened action of body and brain in the interest
of personal power.

So with the disciple who is using the technique.
Once the rhythm of it is established in the vehicles,
there is a steady ascension of life vibration within the
highly organised structure. The soul is dominant;
its own fiery essence is in requisition and is drawn
forth from its secret recesses because the hour of its
need has come. The action of the technique eliminates

all need for specific methods of awakening it. The soulful life of the disciple is the cause of the awakening and the guarantee of its safe manipulation.

What ground have we for affirming that the fire is in evolution in the disciple? Let us think again of the musical artist. We have not a moment's doubt during his interpretation, that the genius of the soul is awakened and in action. It is so evident and arresting that, as we listen, our attention is often forcibly drawn away from the work to the personality of the artist. His magnetic quality opens to us the door to a realm of new creation. We pass out of ourselves, beyond the tyranny of sense and intellect to a rapt contact with the inspirational soul revealed through his work. Words fail us, or all but those that reflect admiration and gratitude for men who can speak the language of the soul which kindles in us the fire that flames at the heart of life. Poor indeed is the man who is not chastened and ennobled by this exhibition of a divine manifestation in the inspired artist. There are few who are not moved by it, even if true appreciation is lacking.

The awakening fire is the note of divinity in the disciple's life, and every avenue of that life's expression reveals it. It plays upon the threefold instrument of his constitution and sets its ineffaceable seal upon body, mind and soul in all their multifarious activities. We can be as sure of this pervading tone of the divine fire in the disciple's life as we can of the inspirational quality in the artist's work, if we have the open mind and the seeing eye. The quality in both is a manifestation of the same energising agent, though directed to different objectives.

But may not the objective of the artist be no less important than that of the disciple on the way? May he not be as beneficent in his intention, as unselfish in his work, and in his influence no less potent than the disciple? Is it not granted that genius is often unconscious discipleship, the master Beethoven being cited as a case in point? All this is true : but I am not attempting a study of relative values of artist and disciple. I cite the creative artist as the most apt illustration of the fire in action to other than a purely spiritual objective. Nowhere else in life shall we find so revealing an illustration of the fire in action as that of the creative artist. And I use it with special intent : for if there is one thing above all others which the artist can teach the disciple, it is that of being completely imbued with the creative spirit and demonstrating the passion of it in all his members. We are left in no doubt about this. It is a condition of entire possession, of the divine afflatus permeating form and subduing it totally to its will to the end of great art and technical expression. The disciple who sets himself the laborious task of mastering the technique of the mystic way may also find his objective and field of service in art, in musical or literary creation ; but whatever his objective, it will be one of conscious and dedicated service which an intensive training has revealed to him. This is so surely the case, that it is difficult to think of an earnest aspirant taking the mystic way, passing the term of meditation, entering upon the contemplative state, and consciously mastering the initial stages of the technique of the soul's expression, without assuming ultimate recognition by a Master and the opportunities of expert tuition for a special sphere in which to devote his maturing consciousness to notable usefulness to his fellowmen.

What characteristics are there in the disciple in whom the fire is awakening, which may be specially noted ? There are several which I believe are always present ; and although characteristics analogous to them may be observed in some individuals of out-standing mental development, there is always a marked difference in the application of them, and further, they will rarely be confused by observant minds. The disciple will manifest a very pro-nounced duality of life and character. This is not difficult to understand when it is remembered that the activity of the fire in him indicates predomin-ance of the soul over the personality—for I am deal-ing only with the case of the disciple in whom the technique itself has awakened the fire, not with forced development for a lesser objective. He actually lives more within the soul sphere than within the personality, and that inevitably ensures a dissociation at will between the two. How will this work out to the view of general observation ? It will manifest in a power of detachment in the dis-ciple's working life which enables him to think, speak and act with complete impersonality regarding issues that confront him. This power of detachment which enables the disciple to function with cool independence of the fact or of personality, is a highly important point. A mystical scripture says : " A disciple will fulfil all the duties of his manhood ; but he will fulfil them according to his own sense of right, and not according to that of any person or

E

body of persons." It means, as said in the writing on the contemplative mind, that the soul has a different set of values than that of the personality and the disciple finds it a matter of necessity to adhere to the one and discountenance the other. There is much responsibility in so doing, and often a great deal is at stake ; but the influence of the fire in him is of that urgency and strength that personal considerations have no voice against it. The mandate of the soul is as clear and peremptory as the swift cognition of mind and vision. For him, it is the soul of things as they are and related to the soul of all, unbiased by the form of personality, that compels allegiance. Few are willing to see it, and if seen, fewer still have the courage to follow it.

It will be seen that this power of detachment and dissociation of the soul from personality issues and hindrances at will, is of itself of an inspirational character. It is really the creative soul working within the personality after the patterns of spiritual truth. It is the artist soul using the instrument of personality and revealing in the process his divine technique. It is direct, relentless and unabating, and imparts rhythm, accent and tone to that personality life. There is no mistaking this : and that is why it may be affirmed that the individual experience of his work and contacts is indubitable proof of the activity in the disciple of the awakening fire. His preparation in the various terms of the mystic way coerces it into living, active response to his purified desire and need. His desire is pure because he loves the soul of man ; and the need is a lawful claim upon the Fire of the Universe to lift that soul to its true estate.

To these two characteristics may be added a third, among many that might be remarked. It is that of fearlessness. Fearlessness in thought, speech and action is not rare among highly mental types : quite the reverse. The strong mental polarisation of the people of the west is responsible for a personal assertiveness and declaration of opinions and views so forcible and wilful, that the Powers behind evolution can no longer remain indifferent to it and seek to avert disastrous consequences from it. But the fearlessness which evolves in the disciple under the action of the fire of the dominant soul, is of a different and higher quality. It has nothing in common with the rude and assertive courage which usually accompanies mental assurance ; it imposes not its strength and authority upon others ; nor is it incompatible with gentleness and compassion and the tears which sorrow and suffering evoke. The fearlessness of the disciple is complete indifference to any consequences which threaten him through following his own light. If the way of preparation has not schooled him to this, something is wanting. The fire has yet to kindle in heart and brain to cleave soul and personality asunder. Until that hour he still waits, whatever his gifts and graces, within the outer court.

CHAPTER VI

THE DARK NIGHT

It was affirmed that the technique of the inner life permitted no sharp demarcation between the mystical and the occult aspects of experience; that there are phases of inner culture and experience and reactions thereto which are common to both. It is well to stress this point here; because, when dealing with intimate phases of soul experience, it is really a confession of one-sided development to insist that one is an occultist and not a mystic, or a mystic but not an occultist. As a student of the literature of mysticism or occultism, he may theoretically call himself an occultist or a mystic; but my submission is, that when he advances to practical research into the life of the soul, he will find a common meeting ground of individual experience. We, even in these days of advancement towards becoming partakers together in a province of universal knowledge, are far too professional and orthodox in what pertains to our little platforms of occult or mystical belief, and are guilty of a pride much lower than spiritual in placing undue emphasis upon the exclusive dignity of our particular platform. This belongs to the life within form. That we

68

denominate it occult or mystical does not alter the fact.

Now, it is very singular that in the literature of occultism there is but cursory if any reference to that momentous phase of inner experience known as the dark night of the soul. Whether it is that the occultist is above being involved in so humiliating an experience, or whether he is so steeled to power and virtue that this experience cannot affect him, or whether, knowing it only too well, he considers it an emotional weakness compatible with the mystical way of the heart but which the head dare not acknowledge, I am at a loss to determine. But so it is : while the most important and formidable phase of experience which every soul must encounter on the way to divine union, is a theme of almost tragic solemnity in all mystical literature, in the literature of occultism there is scarcely passing reference to it. If it were the case that only the aspirant on the mystic way encounters the experience of the dark night, this observation would be irrelevant : but this is not so. If my knowledge of the experience of aspirants is true, one of the greatest burdens I have known arising from this knowledge has come from those who in temperament and development are, and who would acknowledge themselves in their studies to be, students of occultism, not to mention those of a purely mystical type : and that experience has been of the dark night of the soul.

In the face of this conspicuous absence of treatment in occult literature of a major experience in the evolution of the soul, may it not be assumed that it is considered either as a kind of emotional disturbance unworthy of the attention of so dignified a science, or that, in its insistence upon mind control and dynamic assertion of the will as the beginning and end of its technique, any reactions during development of an emotional nature are to be forthwith suppressed and slain, or treated with wilful indifference, the will in all emergencies or crises maintaining a robust domination and carrying the whole life onwards to spiritual conquest ?

A study of psychological types, including special cases of genius and those of a mystical and occult character, will convince an equitable student that the experience of the dark night of the soul awaits every man who approaches the indwelling fire of God ; and this, independently of the fact that he is an occultist, a mystic, a philosopher, or an artist. The name under which he passes or of the path he takes, does not alter the nature of the essential experience, although the particular attitude of the type towards it may to some extent qualify the reactions to it. In proof of this I cite two famous world characters : Pascal and Steiner. In common parlance Pascal would probably be noted as a christian mystic, and Steiner as an occultist. In character they were totally unlike, as they were in method and aim. In scientific technique both were supreme. They were comprehensive thinkers and exact logicians, pioneers in the realms of mind and spirit, and of unsurpassed psychological insight into the profundities of human life and action. Yet both were devotees, perfect in self-abnegation, with a

veritable passion for Christ and the understanding
and beauty of His life and word. If ever the way of
the head and of the heart were united, they were in
these men. Pascal was so possessed with the truth
as it was in Christ that had the great work he wrote
in defence of it appeared in his own name, his brief
life would have been curtailed through persecution.
Steiner was so like Christ that the world adjudged
him a revolutionary, and destroyed one of his
noblest works as a mark of its hatred of him. Name
them as we will, christian, mystic, or occultist, the
shadow of the cross was upon both of them from
first to last, and both carried the agony of the dark
night with them to their grave.

Pascal is a classic example of a man taking the
active and devotional mystic way, or, to otherwise
state it, the middle path, which combines the
occult and mystical aspects of development in a
fervent search after the esoteric truth underlying
the world of phenomena, the world of creative and
spiritual causes, which intuitionally he knew existed
and was ever seeking through the forms of science,
philosophy and religion. I am particularly interested
in the prelude to the revelation he had, as briefly
recorded in his life, because it reveals graphically
the peculiar nature of the dark night as experienced
by him. A year before the revelation he was seized
with an unbearable disgust of the world and all it
could offer him. He applied himself once again with
almost frantic intensity to mathematical investiga-
tions and other scientific pursuits, and to the books
in which he had found his greatest solace—" the old
friends who are never seen with new faces, who are

the same in wealth and in poverty, in glory and obscurity," but they all failed him. The most poignant touch of all is here : " He read his Bible and his books of piety, and found in them more grief than consolation, for they told of the search for salvation which he had abandoned, the love of God which he could feel no more." And, to quote his own words : " If one does not know himself to be full of pride, ambition, concupiscence, weakness, pettiness, injustice, one is very blind. And if, knowing this, a man does not desire to be delivered, what can one say of him ? " There is also that pathetic note of self-revelation made by him : " It is a horrible thing to feel everything one possesses slip away." And once he had written : " If God interrupts however little his mercy, dryness necessarily supervenes." Upon which his biographer comments " Now God had interrupted his mercy, and Pascal had wandered somehow into the desert, peopled only by the mirages of grace." These are the heavy chords in the dark prelude to the revelation by fire.

I have expressed the opinion that within the disciple on the mystic way, who is entering into the various stages of the mystical life of the soul and using its technique, the fire is in process of unconscious awakening and is visibly operative in his work in the world. From the earliest years Pascal showed all the signs of this awakening and use. Wherever he turned the light of his mind, upon science, mathematics and invention, religious philosophy and literary form, there is perceived the mark of the originality, strength and unique creativeness of the fire of the soul. He was an inspirational and creative type, and possessed even in his novitiate these gifts and graces which come only to the few who reach the highest point of the mystic way. Sometimes the scientist held the field, then the religious philosopher, the controversialist, the rapt devotee, as the inspiring fire of the soul inclined ; and during these many essays of genius, the technique of expression of the powers of the soul was raising the life vibration and stimulating the divine heat to a crucial stage of precipitation in the major experience of the way. Then came the interlude of supreme detachment, when the building of years seemed to crumble around him and everything fell away from his grasp. All the brilliance of past achievement became an offence and a burden and passed into eclipse under the consciousness of utter abandonment by God and man.

It may be thought that in citing Pascal I am remarking an exceptional case of genius, to which any degree of approximation cannot be expected. But the same may be thought of Steiner. They were both extraordinary men ; and in their almost tragic lives and in their monumental work, they stand alone. They pushed contemplation to its furthest limits and went out on to " the frightful promontory of thought," and suffered, in and with Christ, the dark night of the soul in extremity. That is the point of my citing these men ; not because they were men of genius, but because they were examples of mystical suffering perfecting human nature and translating it into the divine image. Different from so many angles as their lives were, so different that I doubt

whether they have ever been mentioned in conjunction, yet they show this impressive uniformity
of experience. They were both rich, profoundly
rich, in spiritual emotion ; and for this reason it
probably was that the prolonged experience of the
dark night was so pronounced in them. Steiner's
work, for instance, with all its scientific formality
and architectural beauties, trembles with the passion
of life, known and lived. The same is true of Pascal.
Psychology with its love of classifying all characters,
sacred and profane including that most unclassifiable
of all creations, genius, as introvert and extravert,
would presumably pigeonhole these two men as
introverts, a certain superciliousness of expression
observable in the mystic and the austerity of mien of
the occultist perhaps providing additional and con-
clusive physiognomical testimony for the classification. It could lead us into a painful and unbecoming
and thoroughly hopeless discussion—and prove
nothing. The fact is, that men like Pascal and Steiner
and every other soul who has trodden the secret
way and been tried by fire, who has gone on
before and stands in the silence and solitude of
the shadow of the cross, defy classification. They
are far deeper and more inclusive than anything
they say or do. We can never see these men
whole, because half their lives are in the shadow.
Who can judge the man who has suffered death in
Christ ?

We read much of the mastering of the opposites,
of standing upon a point of balance, poised and aloof
above all the oscillations of life ; and so ambitiously
and conscientiously has this coveted altitude been

striven for, that it is small wonder if a sympathetic and emotional participation in the lives of others should indicate retrogression and a condition of ignoble bondage. But is not a prominent characteristic of the mystic way said to be the power of detachment which enables the disciple to function with cool independence of the factor of personality? That is true. The experience of the dark night effects this transformation in the disciple. It is the supreme trial of all he has brought with him on the way; and this climaxing experience eventuates in the power of detachment. But to conclude that this means an aloofness from and indifference to human life, would be a sad mistake. An alienation from life for the purpose of self-elevation and distinction will never bring an aspirant to the culminating experience of the dark night. He can become an occult theorist of the first magnitude and know all the qualities, with a learned spirit, of occult science, but if he imbues not these with spiritual emotion, and not only so, but fails to convert his knowledge into emotive tendencies and carry them inspirationally as an awakening force into the lives of men, his detachment may be so complete as to ensure him a mournful isolation which no intelligent aspirant would emulate. The detachment of the mystic way dissociates from all that binds the soul from its fullest expression for the good of others and enables it to understandingly identify itself with the struggling life in all forms. It brings the soul into life, enriched and fortified through having sustained the burden of many sorrows of loss, suffering and sacrifice; and recognising that burden in other lives, it willingly shares and seeks to lift it. No man who has experienced the darkness of mystical crucifixion can do otherwise.

Renan, in his *Life of Jesus,* a work which, as is well known, called down upon its author the rage of orthodoxy, dared to reduce the Master from a Divine to a human being, but not an ordinary human being. He depicted Him as a man of superlative genius, a prodigy of religious passion, and wrote of Him with a tenderness and sympathy and profound reverence which elicits our love and admiration. But, while treating the Master Jesus as a transcendent example of compassion and love, of wisdom and clairvoyance, and of unimpeachable probity in speech and action, Renan brought Him down from a pedestal of isolated and unapproachable divinity to the common level of companionship with men and woman, even to the sharing, I do not say in what degree suggested, in the mental and emotional interplay of their manifold vicissitudes and circumstances. I am not interested in why the religionists of Renan's day were so shocked with this portrayal of the Master; but I observe a cogent lesson in it for those on the mystic way, and it points to the condition of participation, and not isolation, to which the experience of the dark night leads the disciple. At this critical juncture of the way, it is not so much a matter of self-initiated effort to achieve, as a forgetting of personal importance and ambition, whether of intellectual or spiritual force, and giving unobstructed permission, within reason, to the interplay of life upon all planes, to a prompt recognition of and reaction to the meaning of life in all forms, to the end of assisting the release and expression of the soul.

It is to be expected that this ideal of mystical participation in human life, which emerges from the dark night of suffering, will have a morbid or senti-mental flavour for those who seek a cheap detach-ment from life in order to escape the suffering incidental to it, by setting up defence barriers which prohibit a sympathetic sharing in it. We should prefer to see the truth as it is. What I see at this point of its evolution is, that human life is steeped in distress and suffering, disillusionment and per-plexity, for all the veneer which struggles to hide it. I sometimes think that the dark night is descending upon a host of souls, under Karmic decree and for a special purpose, instead of upon a few, as in former times, who cultured for it. So much the more in-cumbent is it upon those on the way to accept the tension of life, the cross of circumstances, and the keen thrust of passion upon the sensitive heart, that thereby they may be the sooner called into the light of a larger service to ameliorate with completed experience a suffering world. There will then be no desire to rest, unmoved in mind and emotion, upon the height of self-achievement, blind and unreactive to the kaleidoscope of life below. Mysticism can be a solitary meditation, a pleasing reverie, a benedic-tion for personal gratification, even a passport to a reputation for goodness, of doubtful merit : it can also see and do for others what they need, where they stand. When we see what so-called worldly men sometimes do, in sheer self-forgetfulness, because they have the soul to do it, we may observe with some anxiety so-called discipleship. We regard discipleship as height. So it is : but it is precarious to live in the idea. There is neither height nor depth in real discipleship. It is understanding response to all. That is the mission of the dark night, whatever form it takes in the individual life to reach it. It is the mystical participation of the soul in the world.

CHAPTER VII

MYSTIC LOVE

THE disciple who enters upon the experience of the dark night of the soul, faces the issues of life and death within his own personality. His undeviating ascent on the mystic way is a silent petition to the unseen Powers that he may pass through the darkness of mystical death to all in the personal life that is unworthy to live in the light of Christ. It is a term of adjustment to the values of life, when much is taken away, when much has to be consciously put away, which is a weight and hindrance to the disciple. It is a term of some duration, for the personality is tried in its most vulnerable part and rebels at that which it has evoked. The type of disciple, his native strength and the extent of his past evolution, are determining factors as to the way in which he will pass this term. But whatever changes the purgation of the dark night may work in him, one cardinal virtue will emerge which will be the hall mark of his discipleship : the spirit of mystic love will be born in him, tolerant, kind and long suffering.

It may appear to be a platitude, and a well-worn one, to say that the disciple must be the exponent of love. The orthodox religious life stagnates in platitudes : they provide a safe anodyne for the conscience. But on the mystic way there are some platitudes which are laws of stern necessity. They are basic laws of discipleship. They cease to be formulæ on the tongue and become dictates of the heart. That the disciple must divinely love is one of them. A living compassion for the suffering of our fellowmen is rarely born in us until life has brought us the like experience. And life is so burdened with forms of suffering that few have not some sympathy with it. But how many carry in their hearts and manifest to the world the force and blessing of true mystic love, which is, lest we have forgotten it, in simple truth, the love of Christ ? Small wonder is it that so few emulate what is rarely seen. It is the mission of the mystic to show forth and radiate upon the world that illuminating influence.

During the term of the dark night we seek in vain without for consolation or assistance. It helps us somewhat to ponder the experience of those who have passed through and found the reward of patience and fortitude ; but in the main we are left alone to find our own way. It is not a token of strength and development to rest upon others. That is what the dark night has to teach us. And so searching is the experience, touching the very vitals of life, that, when we are through, there is little in human nature we fail to see the meaning of or cannot rightly appraise, and show compassion for it. The word of Pascal, the face of Steiner, and the anguish of Christ, asking that the cup might be taken from Him, come back to us as striking comments upon "the ingression into the divine shadow," wherein is given personal and experimental knowledge of the sorrow of humanity. For in that which befalls one soul during the term of the dark night, is foreshadowed that which must befall all souls when the hour comes. It is that fore-knowledge, the long-range vision of what must be, which slays hatred in the heart of the disciple, takes away the right and privilege of judgment upon human weakness and error, and instils the spirit of compassion which sees in all the operation and out-working of divine law.

Sympathetic insight into human nature, and a compassionate attitude towards all that this insight reveals, are but one aspect of the experience derived from the dark night; but it is the most important one. It determines and stabilises once for all one's attitude towards others and makes him a forceful influence for good. There are other aspects, of individual significance and benefit which may be noted. There is the liquidation of Karma, which is of prime evolutionary value to the disciple; the liberation from definite personal hindrances which have held him back from a free expression of his deepest self; the consciousness of abiding and imperturbable strength and spiritual reliance arising from the chaos of the personal life; and peace and certitude for the future, because the fire of the soul has raised him to his rightful place of divine sonship. It is therefore an experience which reorients the entire psychology of the disciple. Each aspect of it ramifies deeply into the past and carries its own peculiar psychological and spiritual interest. Obviously then, what we call the dark night is very far

F

from being a term denoting merely an emotional experience which has significance only for an impressionable few of the many on the way. Rather, it is a spiritual privilege offered to the few for which the many on the way are not yet ready. I do not like the word privilege, because on the mystic way there are really no privileges : every step of the way is fought for and won. But I wish to point the fact strongly to the occult theorist, who has yet to learn the value of spiritual emotion, that it is of the nature of a privilege to receive this invitation of the soul to intimate participation in its own inmost life, and he cannot afford to neglect the special spiritually emotive preparation which alone can entitle him to it.

In the chapter on " Mystic Meditation," I referred to the meditation upon the nature of the soul as love, as a foundation for ascent on the mystic way. On looking back to this practice from a more advanced stage the disciple may recognise it as the indispensable cultural and refining influence which has made everything else possible for him. This truth will be accepted by the disciple with complete approval. He knows that love opens all doors on the mystic way. It is from the theorist we may expect criticism, or an attitude of indifference. Of all the persons who suffer from inhibitions and repressions and all the other complexes which psychology has discovered in these latter days, the occult theorist is often a classic example. His intention is good and he means well, but he is so bent upon focusing the life energies inward for self-development, that even the most normal expression of the emotional nature carries with it moral censure. One-pointed concentration is his gospel, and if he deviates one step from it, he is lost. " But ye have not so learned Christ." Not all the concentration in the world will bring us so near to Christ as the following of that which Pascal and Steiner saw in Him. This is a hint for all of us on the mystic way. We may concentrate until our skulls crack in perfect detachment : it will not give us one heart throb of the divine fervour which made Christ and these disciples perfect servants.

I have come to the conclusion, through close contact with the lives of a large number of aspirants, that many of them are really afraid of the expression of love in the mystic sense. Within the narrow limits of a personal relationship they may know the power and value of love in their lives, but so far as mystical love participation in other lives is concerned, they are sleeping souls. This is an observable and regrettable fact. The causes of this inhibited love expression are many and various, and of too remote yet intimate and psychological a nature to be discussed here. It is only possible to refer to a prevailing condition among aspirants. Each has his own problem, and individual study and reflection can solve it. In some aspirants, it must be said, the refusal of mystical participation is a sublimated form of selfishness. The remedy lies in deliverance from the bondage of their own will. The ideas about will and control freely imbibed from Eastern literature are the cause of half the failures on the mystic way, or the cause of so few reaching the goal of their desire on the way. Their primary need is to learn, with true understanding and humility, the surrender of the will, that the blessing they have so far received on the way may pass into human hearts. The love of the soul which should flow forth freely upon all, is circumscribed and turned back upon themselves in meticulous thoughtfulness to ensure self-development. As a purely mental exercise this has its value, but it has no mystical significance. It is as alien to the life of Christ and the Masters as is the calculated self-consideration of those professed religionists whose religion is a veneer to cover the intents and purposes of an irreligious soul. Is it any wonder that unselfish souls who know nothing of the way do the most to bless and uplift their fellowmen? I know these are hard words; but the impeachments of Christ were harder and true. The word of Christ was the most destructive ever launched against mankind during two thousand years. But there was a constructive influence behind it. The basic concepts implanted by Him in human consciousness were the sacredness and value of individuality and the necessity for individual effort towards ascension in consciousness; the idea of the oneness of humanity through the realisation of the indwelling soul; and mystical participation in the lives of others through love. In a word, He taught individual responsibility, that by his own personal effort alone can one attain to divinity; that the same opportunity of mystical realisation was open to all men; and that through mystical participation through love identification with Himself and all souls should climax the mystic way. It is a very old theme. If the orthodox religionist has forgotten the import of it, or has never been taught it, there is no excuse for the aspirant on the way. He has personally to accept this teaching laid down by Christ and work out the concepts of it to the letter in all its implications in his own life. It is of little merit in him to regard with legitimate disgust institutional religion, that chequered state passport to social position and professional prestige, if he has nothing more virile and worthy of emulation to put in its place.

It has been said that the degree of love in a man is the measure of his genius, and the degree of his self-seeking is the measure of his narrow-mindedness. There is a deep esoteric truth here. The disciple on the way accepts and exemplifies in his life the three concepts of the Christ life mentioned above. He accepts individual responsibility for development in taking the various mystical stages; in the contemplative stage he contacts the nature of the soul and manifests it in world service; and ultimately he seeks identification with all souls through mystic love. This last stage is in a high degree technical and calls for a good deal of inward discipline. The measure of his genius on the way will be according to his love, and no purely mental or occult discipline will alter the fact, nor will anything else take the place of it. I have known disciples of great promise and possessing mystical gifts that placed them far ahead of their fellows in evolution, but they failed in one thing, and this compelled them to pause as before a closed door: they had not realised the value, potency and absolute necessity of crowning their long labours with the mystic love which leads to identification with Christ and all souls. No matter how lofty the soul, or how true it is to its discipline,

until it has become wholly merciful, softened and
suffused with mystic love for all, dying to its own
will that others may rise through its abnegation and
self-forgetfulness, it cannot pass on and stand in the
presence of those who have made the last surrender.
It is profoundly true that the degree of one's self
seeking is the measure of his narrow-mindedness,
even though that narrow-mindedness may be on a
far higher level than what we usually think of when
we speak of narrow-mindedness in common parlance. Why is this? Because identification with other
souls through mystic love participation can only
come through inspirational sensitivity to souls. How
can we truly assist the evolution of souls if we cannot enter into the inmost nature of the soul? Many
students pride themselves upon their knowledge
of others through the exercise of certain occult arts,
which is no doubt very interesting and diverting,
possibly informative. But the soul is an original
and divine entity and stands aloof from all stereo-
typed calculations that would mark its passage and
influence. It is little less profane than judging of the
the soul of a man by the contours of his face. The
disciple may legitimately use these adjuncts of
knowledge in his service to others, but he will never
regard them as basic and decisive. Inspirational sensitivity to the atmosphere and nature of the soul is
the way of entrance and understanding, and this is
only unfolded through love. Love is the attractive
and revealing quality of the soul and is the only key
to other souls. The terms of ascent on the way
should result, if purposefully undertaken, in an increasing sensitivity to life in all forms. The more

the disciple withdraws into himself in consecrated living, the more sympathetically must he enter into other lives : the two conditions are coetaneous on the way. The deeper the knowledge of his own soul, the more profound his knowledge of and mystical participation in the life of other souls. This entrance and participation must be so real and vital that the problem of another soul, its quality, tendency and possibility, must have equal claim upon him with that which concerns himself. It is this attitude of living in and with other souls which develops in the disciple an inspirational inclusiveness, gives an un-erring insight into their psychology, and inspires him to right thought and action in their behalf. Through this sensitivity the disciple reads the psy-chology of the soul, which let it be said, is very far removed from a prurient psycho-analysis and the psychology of the schools. Mystic love has no place in the exercise of the technique of the latter, pene-trating and revealing as it is. An acute and dis-criminating intellect may master it with ease, and apply it honourably and usefully, but only within the limits of its soulless domain. Indeed, it is only too often as much in need of a soul psychology to clarify its own views and conclusions as are those whom it essays to enlighten.

The true psychology of the soul which inspira-tional sensitivity reveals to the disciple through mystic love participation, leads to the identification or oneness with all souls as inculcated by Christ. That is the high point of the mystic way we are con-sidering. It is not easy of attainment, but the cul-mination of long interior discipline in which love is the guiding light. But should not emphasis be laid upon impersonal love? Impersonal love! How deeply, seriously, and wholly onesidedly have aspirants taken to heart the doctrine of impersonal love. How they have endeavoured to slay their poor, hungering, mortal selves, because the Masters are said to be beyond personality and unmoved by human passion. I do not believe it. If I did, I should still think the aspirant a misguided person in trying to play the Master while he is yet merely a disciple in the making. A little right perspective on the way is such a gracious possession, and a real blessing to one's fellows. I have every sympathy with an aspirant who has so religiously imbibed the doctrine of impersonal love as being the only possible way of attainment, that he has forgotten what love is. He may say, nevertheless, that it is one of the most perplexing problems he has to deal with. I grant it may be perplexing; but there is usually something blindly selfish in the background of it. If there is anything this world needs it is love, personal love, the love of Christ. His love, it seems to me, was personal enough. I think the people He consorted with are ample proof of that. He loved men and women, that is all; and He insisted upon the love of men and women, without distinction or reservation, as the one way of mystical realisation of the kingdom of the soul. The impersonal love of many half-educated aspirants is grounded upon a refined selfishness, or a reprehensible self-righteousness. And when it is grounded upon neither of these, it is grounded upon an abject fear to express what throbs and aches within their own heart. Well, those are self-erected barriers which must fall before the soul can ever know itself, not to mention entering upon the stage of mystical participation with other souls. It was said that these barriers or inhibitions of various kinds are of too intimate and psychological a nature to be discussed at length. Obviously they differ in every case. But the resolution of this problem is precisely that which calls for the interior discipline mentioned. No disciple attains to the richness and fullness of the love of Christ without long probation. It is a studied pilgrimage with infinite necessary adjustments and readjustments, during which his many Karmic attachments and responsibilities are brought forth to the light of day by the fire working within him. If he is fully aware of his task and thoroughly prepared for it, he will accept, with patience and understanding, all that is involved in the orientation of his affectional life. The disciple who is advanced in the technique of the way will not be long delayed at this stage. The awakening fire will have reached a point of ascension and force in him which will swiftly release him from the inhibitions referred to. For observe, this release to mystical love participation is bound up with the attitude of fearlessness in regard to all personal considerations in following his own light. It is consideration for opinions, other people's opinions, which is mainly responsible, in this particular connection, for the non-participation which holds some disciples back from completion of experience. But a refusal to follow that which Karma prompts him to and makes possible in a particular cycle, is by no means an unusual condition, even in the case of a disciple. On the contrary, it is sometimes the most promising disciples, as said, who, with all their knowledge and many abilities are held back from their highest objective because they fail to participate understandingly and willingly in the mystic love experience. Not that they are blind to this fact. Indeed, they suffer under the knowledge of it. There are intimate, psychological causes, of an inhibitory nature, set up in a former cycle, which deter them from complete life expression by their invisible bonds. Yet when the fire within has reached its strength, nothing of past or present will have power to stand against it. The true disciple will know that the essence of that fire is love itself and the soul energetic and expressive ; and the soul so released from bondage by the example of Christ, will love after its own law, sanely, sublimely and inclusively.

CHAPTER VIII

MYSTICAL PARTICIPATION

MYSTICAL participation has been defined, in the words of a psychologist, as " merely a relic of the original, psychological non-differentiation of subject and object, hence of the primordial unconscious state ; it is therefore a characteristic of the early infantile mental condition." As an example of original psychological definition, this is an excellent one ; but the reader will have a very different one in mind in its application to the mental condition of the mystic. The truth is, that when the latter has taken a few decisive steps on the way, psychology loses track of him and seeks to account for his absence in an " archaic collective unconsciousness." Again, we have been told that mystical participation is also " a characteristic of the unconscious content in adult civilised man, which, in so far as it has not become a conscious content, remains permanently in the state of identity with objects." Even so, the reader may think, with me, that there is nothing necessarily mystical in a man identifying himself with objects. If there is, I submit there is some difference between identification of an untutored savage with objects and that enlightened mystical participation of a civilised man who spiritually identifies himself with his fellowmen, and perhaps with the world of nature, too.

That queer but brilliant genius, Rousseau, had something interesting to say in this connection. " We cling to everything, we clutch on to all times, places, men, things ; all that is, and all that will be, matters to each of us ; our individual self is only the least part of ourselves. Each extends, as it were, over the whole earth, and becomes sensitive to this whole vast surface." Rousseau, obsessed, misunderstood and ostracised, was not far from the truth of the mystic way. He was very near it. Psychology does not think so. It says that, " What Rousseau depicts is nothing but that primitive collective mentality of mystical participation, a residue of that archaic time when there was no individuality whatsoever." So much for the findings of psychology. Clearly, we should look in vain to it for an understanding and interpretation of the technique of the mystic way.

While we should not look to Rousseau for an exposition of the way, he, like many other pioneers in the world of thought whose ideas have influenced generations of thinkers, often wrote inspirationally, and with true mystical insight depicted the condition of mystical participation which is sought by the disciple on the way. " Each extends, as it were, over the whole earth, and becomes sensitive to this whole vast surface." If this quotation is considered unfortunate, as coming from the work of a man who was an eccentric and suffered for years in solitude under a persecutional mania, let it be said that I choose it deliberately because psychology has chosen it and assured us that the product of this man's reveries was nothing but " that primitive collective mentality of mystical participation." Presumably, therefore, it would assign the rich products of the reveries of Emerson, Whitman, and a host of other souls of rare mystical insight, to " an early infantile mental condition." A contemporary writer has said that " Theology took the spirit away from religion, and psychology has taken away its soul." It is true. But what neither has done, and never will do, is to take away the soul from mysticism. Both will have to come to mysticism to solve their ultimate problems, and many preliminary ones.

Now, to turn again to serious ground, it is just this exceptional sensitivity, which enables one to extend, as it were, over the whole earth, and become aware of the whole, that characterises the condition of the disciple in the advanced stages of the way ; which invites and compels him to a mystical participation in the life of the entire living organism of which he is a conscious part. To accept this position intellectually is not enough : he has to feel into, intuit and know through the energising force of the love of the soul released within himself, the latent and developing soul life in all. Mystical participation does not consist in the ordinary manifold contacts of everyday life, however strong and consolidated these may be. It emerges upon a far higher and more interior level of consciousness, as a result of having taken the stages of mystical discipline. It is Christ ministering to the world through the members of His own body, when these have been trained to do His will. It means that the disciple has so far transferred the focus of his life from the plane of personality to that of the indwelling soul, that it is habitual with him to pass beyond the personality in others and contact the soul life within them. As the personality has its specific aura which conveys to the sensitive its prevailing note and characteristics, so has the soul its sounding quality which conveys to the disciple its vibratory measure of tone, depth and status whereby it is recognised and known. But even that contactual knowledge is not necessarily mystical participation. No : but such an intimate knowledge of the soul dawning upon the disciple's consciousness under the influence of a noble and unselfish love born within him through his long novitiate, inevitably prompts him to regard that soul as a sacred entity with an immortal destiny, carrying within itself the like promise of discipleship and masterhood. If he has not that love he may still read, but his sight will be coloured and he will read amiss. Some do so read, for personal ends, and their mental bias is reflected in their reading. Instead of redeeming a soul they increase its bondage. That is not the work of a disciple, but of an interloper essaying the way with the exercise of occult art. His failure is written, not in his stars, but in himself.

The disciple, bearing ever within himself the memory of past struggles and failures, of heavy days and nights of intolerable darkness, of fears, hopes and conquests, and softened and matured under the impresses of this searching experience, but above all, understanding the action, reaction and interplay of these many militant factors which the soul has to face and adjust to in the personal life, does in truth mystically participate in and live with other souls through the storied drama of their evolution. Mystical participation is then a spiritual condition, following upon spiritual cognition, which is a faculty of developed soul consciousness. It is neither subnormal, an example of " collective unconscious emergence of a primitive character " ; nor abnormal, a condition calling for pathological treatment ; but supernormal and divine, using as its technique a psychology operating after the laws of mystical consciousness.

There is a positive and a negative aspect in the exercise of mystical participation. The negative aspect is likely to furnish a problem to some disciples who are unusually expansive and inclusive in their mental and emotional life. Where this condition exists there is a tendency in the disciple to be so fluid and absorptive as to lose the strength and stability of individuality necessary for true helpfulness. This can go so far as to prove a deterrent rather than a help to himself and others, in that he unwittingly assumes responsibility which it is of first importance to others they should carry in the interest of their own evolution. It is right for him to lift to the measure of his strength something of the heavy Karma of the world ; but the positive aspect of participation is needed for that, and it is rooted in self poise. Mystical participation is not sentimental emotionalism : it is grounded upon self-contained individuality and guided by clear seeing wisdom and practical action. This distinguishes the

mystic of the middle way from many instances
furnished by mystical biography which we read with
some misgiving. They are of participation of a
passive, overwrought and unhealthy type, in their
degree unselfish, meritorious and influential, but
lacking the real technical equipment of discipleship.

The tendency towards a positive or negative type
of participation will be determined by the type of
disciple exercising it. The psychology of the schools
classifies the mental types broadly as introvert and
extravert. There is something analagous to this
classification in the two types of disciples in their
mystical participation in other lives. The mental
introvert on the way will be the disciple using the
positive aspect of participation. The love force in
him will be no less powerful through his training
than in his opposite, the mental extravert on the way
using the passive aspect of participation. But the
former will manifest a marked self-containment of
individuality and prove of outstanding inspirational
force and strength in his contacts : the latter will
have the attractive magnetism and healing quality
which infuses itself with a spontaneous lavishness
which is apt to ignore in his contacts the basic
factors of time and circumstance. But those factors
are of primary importance in service, and if they are
neglected the best results of participation will not
ensue.

I have known disciples of both types on the way
and studied the values and hindrances incident to
each respectively. The values of the one type have
been sometimes lessened because its mental intro-
version has modified unduly the affectional interplay

in other lives. Its inspirational quality has been high and stimulating, its power of entrance into the soul life of others unchallengeable, yet because of a long established habit of self-involvement and dissociation, although with laudable motives, the magnetic and affectional interplay with others has been restricted and curtailed its highest value in service. The hindrances of the other type have arisen from causes of an opposite nature. Its magnetic and fusing quality has been of so free, fluent and discursive a character, so inclusive and possessive, that the integrity of individuality necessary for eliciting the best in others has been weakened and led to disappointment through unlooked for complications in its contacts.

It is this negative aspect of participation which characterised many mystics of the past, so much so that it is not surprising they have been considered pathological cases. But with our greater knowledge of the mechanics of the soul and the technique of its evolution, there is afforded every facility for uniting the best in both types of head and heart, the mental and the magnetic in a harmonious development on the way. Indeed, for the achievement of high initiated consciousness this is imperative. The basic laws of the inner life remain the same as hitherto, but evolution has moved on rapidly and the disciple of to-day has a far different problem before him in service than in the past. Exaggerated development in any part of his equipment must be rounded off and a stable balance achieved. He must be far too manifestly sane, practical and understanding in all his contacts, whether in ordinary or in mystical

G

participation, to be considered abnormal and pathological. But not in order to avoid criticism : that does not count : but to meet the exacting exigencies of his time. The world calls for that type of disciple, and he must be forthcoming. He is forthcoming ; but more are needed. The object of this book is to stimulate the interest of those who are capable of this discipleship.

Let us consider further the value of and the possible hindrance to mystical participation. I have had so many experiences of the value of it in other lives that a volume would be required to recount them. Disciples of the mystic way know the meaning of the word suffering and do not turn from it as a depressing theme. They know that it is intimately bound up with the mystical life : for it is precisely those on the way who are called upon to suffer ; and if it is not their own suffering, then through their own developing sensitivity they are sympathetically drawn to share in that of others. That is the penalty, far rather the privilege, of entering upon the way. There is no avoiding it. As certainly as the disciple proceeds along the way will he enter into the suffering of human life. But what is there in this life of more value than trying " to lift a little of the heavy Karma of the world ? " There is no greater reward than the heart-spoken gratitude of those whose suffering we have made our own through passing through the shadow in soul with them. Do not retreat from it, but let the scars of human sorrow remain in the soul as a lasting memorial of your compassion and kindness. It is the one thing the Master waits to read there. It is the

universal language of Masters and disciples, the
mystic bond which unites them into one compassionate fraternity. For what is the ground of the
solicitude of the Master, the watchful care which
he exercises in training his pupil to share in his own
work? Not assuredly to satisfy any personal
motives of the disciple, least of all to meet a personal
desire for special powers to demonstrate his ascen-
dancy over his fellow men. It is for one reason only :
to share the burden of the Karma of the world.
That is the purpose of the way. It is a call to the
disciple to enter experimentally into the mystery of
the cross which lies athwart the path of life. In so
doing he is led to the heart of that mystery and
becomes a conscious participator in the compassionate life of the Masters.

One of the chief hindrances to mystical participation to be met with, even in those advanced on the
way, is fear. They may repudiate the assertion, but
it is true. In fact, it is the stronger in them than in
the average individual because accentuated through
the special training they have undergone. The fear
which was once a factor in the objective life is re-
born in the psychic life and functions there as a
retarding influence until driven out by love. And
this is the ignoble way in which it operates : the
growth of personal power and prestige which the
disciple's training inevitably unfolds in him, has a
tendency to raise up with it a sense of superiority
and aloofness which makes him unwilling to share
his self with others. I say unwilling, but it is more
correct to say, makes him fear participation in the lives
of others. There is a rooted fear of self-expression,

potent and not fully recognised. There is such a thing as standing on one's dignity on the way; and if there is anything certain to make one stand instead of progress, this dignity, or fear of self-expression, will do it. Why should a disciple be afraid to express what is in him? What, after all the counting of our virtues and abilities, is the value of this sense of dignity and superiority? It is a very real thing in some disciples, or I could not write of it: but wherever it is found, there, I am sure, a profound and comprehensive nature is lacking. That is just the point. Participation in human life, an intimate contact with its perplexities, sorrow and suffering, is the only way to that depth and fullness of nature which makes a disciple the friend of souls. So long as he stands back within himself, I do not care how noble his character or rare his virtues, and refuses the healing of his loving hands and heart to those who wait for it, he stagnates in his own all-sufficient goodness, which is good for nothing. It is a sorry thing to see a man on the way, bound hand and foot within the narrow circle of his own goodness, and afraid to use and express the very life born within him by his own effort because he may be misunderstood and ill-judged.

What is the root cause of this fear in a knowledgeable man on the way? I submit that it inheres in one of his strongest virtues, that it is rooted in the very strength of his individuality. It is written that " Each man is to himself absolutely the way, the truth, and the life. But he is only so when he grasps his own individuality firmly. . . ." There are disciples so constituted that they take that scripture all too literally. They take every means to foreclose themselves against all impression or assault from without. They build an individuality four-square, and, it is hoped, invulnerable; the ramparts are so high that they can neither themselves get out nor can anyone else get in. That is their individuality at its best. Who can question the value of it? Not I, remembering how few individuals there are even on the way. I admit fully that anything that menaces the integrity of individuality is worth instant scrutiny; and in view of the many influences, in persons and circumstances, that do menace it, not only are they worth instant scrutiny, but challenge and forthright opposition. The disciple who has not the spirit of challenge and opposition in him will not get far on the way in this world. Has not the disciple been called a battle-scarred warrior? He has acquired that title because he has had to hold the ramparts of his individuality so often and tenaciously against the onslaught of influences on more than one plane of life. Why does the same scripture speak of warfare in a true militaristic nomenclature; of the battlefield exhorting the disciple to " look for the warrior, and let him fight in him ? " Why, if not that the building of the ramparts of a powerful individuality is necessitated through the incessant attack of seen and unseen influences which would make violent inroads upon it to its destruction unless challenged and opposed by the warrior within? That is one aspect of individuality, and it cannot be overlooked.

The other aspect, which constitutes a hindrance to the disciple towards mystical participation is, that with large experience of this menace to his individuality, he remains foreclosed within its ramparts and fears to venture out and beyond them in case he may lose his hard won possession. This is one of the major problems of the way for the disciple who has found his strength and fears to lose it. But it is a strength that fears the final trial of itself. He must be strong enough to go forth and enter into other lives with a wise forgetfulness of himself. The challenge and the opposition must still be there, keen, strong and self-contained; but if he is perfected in love, that will be his armour. His individuality will now take care of itself. He can go forth at will and participate in life to the full, without fear of loss and with little thought of former foes. They have done their worst, and been repulsed. The Master will read, in good time, many wounds upon the fair face of the soul; but there will be a light upon it showing clearly how the battle has gone. The disciple who carries no signs of battle has nothing to rejoice over; but it is the inner eye alone that reads the history of them; and they determine his future status. But the battle must have been won for something: self conquest is not the end of it. That is where a disciple sometimes stands, in happy recollection of that. It is not enough. He has to come forth from his individuality, with the magnetism of fearless love about him which can traverse the battlefield unharmed because in spirit and action he is harmless, and can kneel in compassion beside many a suffering son of man who scarcely knows the meaning of individuality and has no retreat from the strife of the day.

CHAPTER IX

THE DISCIPLE MILITANT

I WONDER how many aspirants, when entering upon
the novitiate of the mystic way, realise that they are
actually in training for a spiritual campaign. How
many, of those who set forth with the most varied
hopes of unusual works and achievements, know
that they are candidates for a life of ordeal and battle?
Militancy is the very last term they would be inclined
to associate with the way of discipleship. I would
make it one of the first. What is more common than
to speak of the battle of life, the struggle for supremacy, the seizure of opportunity, the wilful endeavour
to hold one's own in the rushing tide of affairs?
True, the aspirant may say, but this is definitely of
the world, worldly, and we cannot speak of the life
of discipleship in these terms. But all that is operative on the lower plane of life in this respect is
operative on the higher: the same faculties and
forces are brought into requisition on the one plane
as on the other, only under transmutation and with a
new direction. If a man has a fine mental courage
in all the circumstances and affairs of life, is he, as a
spiritual aspirant, to relinquish this splendid acquisition, soften and emasculate the spirit of a masterful

mentality and fear to utter the truth he knows because he may give offence or incur the opposition of little minds ?

There is an important truth here that many aspirants need to ponder. Once on the way and under instruction, they turn the edge of some of their best qualities and fear to be themselves. They become changed for good and for ill simultaneously. They have a higher outlook and a weaker grip on things around them. There are two causes responsible for this, in my opinion. One is, that they apply the art of transmutation so far that it becomes a vice. With them, all on the mental plane must become spiritual. Everything in them has to fall into a subdued key to point the difference between the objective and the mystical life. They are so conscious of their art that they cease to be natural in the use of it. Instead of giving them freer expression it impairs their every movement, through fear of making a false step. Their conscientiousness knows no bounds, and prevents even a normal adjustment to their fellowmen. They are out of focus with themselves and the world. Their transmutation means shrunken faculties instead of expanded ones, and takes them away from human life and not more understandingly into it. The articles of the church they heartily abjure, but they have a set of their own almost as useless. They forget that soul culture is to free the faculties to higher and larger expression, not to put them into another kind of bondage. The word of power they once spoke with perfect abandon they now consider irreligious and prohibited ; and inspiration loses its voice on the way of peace.

There is another reason, and I do not know which is more to be deprecated. Once on the way and they think they are under the surveillance of a Master mind who notes every word they utter and thing they do. The ideas they cherish on this matter are astounding and ridiculous. It argues a tremendous conceit in an aspirant to consider himself so important as to be watched twenty-four hours of the day by the hierarchy. I am sure the personal pupil of a Master would not expect quite so much consideration : if he did he would not get it. It is not the idea of seeking guidance that is out of joint : it is looking for it without instead of within, and to a Master mind from whom the aspirant's development gives no warranty of special supervision. And this attitude of passive dependence has a pernicious effect upon his faculties ; for, so far from being a recipient of a Master's supervision, he is but a slave to his own thought creations and amenable to suggestions from them. The Master does not use this type of material : the force of his vibration would shatter it ; and it is to point this fact that I have made these comments. If the aspirant could realise, which is impossible therefore he must take the word on faith, the nature of that vibration in its strength, rhythm and tone, he would be no longer in doubt as to what type of individual he must be to bear the force of it.

We can look to the example of Christ for all things pertaining to the way, and in Him we see a warrior of the first magnitude. I challenge anyone to with the 23rd chapter of Saint Matthew, for instance, readout recognising that he is face to face with a puissant, aggressive spirit trained to warfare and skilled in the highest degree in the use of the weapons which made Him a deadly antagonist of those men and forces which He knew to be the avowed enemies of His mission. The humility, gentleness and compassion of Christ we love to dwell upon, and it is well; but that is only one aspect of His manifold nature and masterhood, and alone would never have fulfilled His mission. His austerity of speech and directness of action, His unqualified utterances of rebuke and criticism, His swift exposure of subtle and hidden influences working against Him, and His cool indifference to all consequences, give a vivid impression of the militant spirit engaged in conscious combat with the principalities and powers arrayed against him. If we accept one aspect of this great character, we must accept the others, or place Him in a false light and deprive ourselves of half its force and inspirational value. The deeper I read into the Christ life the more conscious I am of the tremendous reserve militant force in it. Where else shall we look for such pathetic entreaties to love, peace and godliness: where else for such unexpected blows struck for these upon those who were enemies to them ? Indeed, one of the most dramatic effects of the scripture records is the surprise and consternation caused by His speech and action upon those who sought to impose upon Him and thwart His mission.

Again, we have only to turn to fragments of mystical teaching on the way to meet at every step the same tone of militancy. " Beware of doubt "; " beware of fear "; " beware of the

lethal shade "; " hold firm "; " have mastery ";
" beware of change ": " again and again the battle
must be fought and won." Why all these exhortations to preparation for battle and to battle itself
if there are not potent and menacing forces ranged
in the way of advance which require coolness,
circumspection, toughness of fibre, challenge and
unrelenting opposition to overcome them ? These
master teachings of the scriptures are founded
upon the truth of the way, and symbolical as
they often are, only point the truth the more
graphically.

Let us descend a step from the scripture to the
master artist, Beethoven, who was scripture embodied, although I may be harshly judged for saying
so. " There is Satan in this young man," said a
contemporary of the master. Well, if the devil was
in him it made short work of his enemies and carved
a clear path for the good God to thunder through
him the music of the spheres. Beethoven was a
creative disciple, and that is just why he possessed
a militant spirit. This is not to say that the disciple
must be possessed of the devil to do his best work ;
but I do say he will never be a creative disciple or
do much for the world unless he has a militant
spirit.

The aspirant must prepare for these paradoxes
of the way. It is a many-sided figure he has to study
and adjust to that reflects the truth of the way. We
have spoken of love, of the beauty and value of its
perfected expression in the highly evolved disciple ;
but it has to be fought for like every other possession
on the way. The love needed is the spirit of God

in action in man, and that is a most potent and searching energy, nothing less, in fact, than a two-edged sword. The fire of the spirit : that is the note of our theme. That is the note of the conquering disciple. It strikes forth from the word of Christ with awful effect. It glances along the line of every scripture of the way. It breaks forth at every step true genius takes. I feel the momentum of it through the ages to the present day : the dynamic and militant spirit of God in action in worthy men who surrendered all to be the living exponents of it. Is it too much to expect that the disciple should be trained to this same warfare of the spirit in action in a dedicated personality ? And observe, it is a perfected love that brings the warrior to his best estate. There is nothing contradictory in this. The love of some aspirants is like a poet's dream, a beautiful thing to contemplate on a summer's day, but totally useless for the rigours of the high altitudes of the way. There is nothing in this world that has such grim opposition as the influence of perfected love in man ; that is why it needs to be militant, challenging and unrelenting in its onward march. The reason is not far to seek. Perfected love is in possession of a kingdom whose forces threaten the foundations of the realms of hate, greed and selfishness established all too firmly upon the objective and the inner planes of life ; and the forces of those realms are ranged against every son of man of dedicated soul and idealistic purpose. It was the forces of these realms that Christ constantly challenged and openly denounced because He knew they were intent upon the destruction of

the work of His hands.   So in Beethoven, consciously possessed of the creative spirit itself, we
see the perfected love of the artist for a divine
mission casting headlong all, even his own physical
infirmities, that dared to oppose the grandest
expression of it.   And in the disciple, if he has
perfected his technique, there must be the same
conquering force of the dominant spirit of militant
opposition against the forces of glamour and decep-
tion [and other menacing influences that would
weaken his power and purpose in the service of his
fellowmen.

My object is to awaken the aspirant to a sense of
the magnitude of the task before him.   At the
beginning of the way it is easy travelling.   He is
enamoured with the newness of the way ; he has a
pleasant sense of entering into new knowledge,
and, shall we say, of taking a few steps in advance,
of his time ; all of which is well and does no harm,
provided he continues onward.   It is not until he
falls into a steady pace and demands the greater
things that his soul tries him out.   This has been
touched upon in another place.   Here we are
thinking of the disciple at the meridian, he who
stands on the right hand of the Master and who knows
what a precarious position that is.   Is it then a life
of trial from first to last, it may be asked, even when
a disciple stands near to the Master ?   I am afraid
it is, and a very severe one.   A student suggested
to me that the reward of the way might be given a
place.   But what reward can we speak of on the way
except the consciousness of a growing technique
to be of value in the world ?   The disciple I am

thinking of is troubled very little about the matter of rewards on the way. He is a man who has tasted many rewards that the world can give, and they have lost their savour. Nearly all these rewards belong to the personal and ambitious life, and his interest is not now focused there. If they come he will use them in the interest of the greater service he has at heart; but he will not seek them. I do not know any greater reward than that the disciple should find himself, through labour, trial and long devotion, a recognised force in the fraternity of the lovers of souls who have made themselves worthy to stand on the right hand of the Master. Life is then forthright, no matter how difficult, because the whole host of lesser desires and ambitions, which chain men to the earth and to repeated rebirth to sorrow and suffering until these are surrendered, no longer dominate the soul and enforce its bondage. Even so, the trial of the disciple is a very real one. Observe the exhortations I have quoted from the scriptures. Are these for naught? Look around and into human life, and no one more clearly than the disciple can see how the face of it is darkened with the shadows that betray the existence of forces diametrically opposed to all he is and stands for. These are the sworn foes of the spiritual man on the material and psychic levels of life, and they look for his downfall and strive for it. The greatest foes of the disciple are arrayed against him on the material and psychic levels. It is there they work in power and in silence to mislead and dishearten and dismay the solitary warrior here and there among men. The trial comes through the height of man. Height in the disciple means extreme sensitivity to influences in the three worlds of form, material, psychic and mental ; and when these combined forces impinge upon the sensitive consciousness, can the life be other than one of trial ?

Hence the need for the militant spirit in the disciple. With the range of receptivity on all levels rapidly increasing, he is drawn to the centre of a veritable battlefield of forces working for good and ill, and he has to hold in steady equilibrium the one and neutralise the other. He is wide open to the reception of both, and the fine art of his technique is to register and discriminate the quality, value and purpose of that which his sensitive receiving apparatus records. He is a lighted beacon in the inner world, drawing to himself by irresistible magnetic love the light and leading of great souls who stand in the vanguard of the battle for spiritual supremacy ; he is also the well-considered target of the hell-born forces that use their black art in skilfully contrived machinations to quench the light that falls upon their secret councils of darkness and exposes them. It is by virtue of the protecting grace of the Master that the disciple is able to bring those machinations to naught. That grace gives light and a puissant force which discerns the adversary and disarms his strongest attack. The adversary takes many shapes, and this is well, for otherwise the eye and judgment would never become keen and sure to discern it. This is part of the disciple's highest training. Under a merciful law it is only he, and not the aspirant feeling his way, who has to face this keenest of trials. The unsure aspirant has little menace for the forces that work against evolution. The momentum of his life is not yet strong enough to sound a note of warning in their realms. It is not until his soul has written its pledge before the Master's eye and his step is strong and sure on the way, his will is set and his heart dedicated to the highest service at any cost, it is not until then that the sounding quality of his life stirs the dark forces to action against him. And instances abound among disciples of this dark encounter, so unseen, veiled and insidious, that the hardest of tasks is to convince them that their own aspiration and dedication are the root cause of the trial. The adversary takes many shapes, in persons and circumstances. If this were not so, what hope could there be of discipleship and masterhood ? That the Master can guide the disciple through all the intricacies of soul evolution is proof that he knows experimentally every aspect of the trial. That the disciple stands near to the Master is proof that he has accepted the challenge of the trial, and has so far won. Let the aspirant remember this and take courage.

I say, so far won : for the disciple near to the Master has much to do. It is some commendation to be near and have the protection and guidance of the Master ; it means that the militant spirit of the disciple has brought him so far, the militant spirit guided by love. How much he has to do before he becomes like the Master ! What constitutes his greatest trial at this point ? That he, like the aspirant, has his Karma to adjust ; but unlike the latter, the disciple's adjustment is swifter and made under pressure. He has no time to waste or palter with the issues ; he is of value in evolution and, under his own voluntary pledge to the Higher Powers, he is taken at his word and brought swiftly to door after door of crisis and opportunity. As a disciple he has many assets : as a human being he has many liabilities. The balance must be adjusted before he may enter into the Kingdom of Christ. Precisely what those liabilities are he will scarcely realise himself, but they will be presented to him, in human contacts and circumstances. These challenging influences, clothed in human form and opposing circumstances, are like elongated shadows showing the uneven contours of the past and falling between him and the Master's perfected life. I would not dare say that he needs here the puissant, militant and challenging spirit above all things, except for one consideration : that during the terms of novitiate, he has cultivated in high degree those qualities of discipleship often referred to, and pre-eminently, compassion, tolerance and love. Without these, the militant spirit alone would raise in him a personal force of a destructive character, a menace to himself and others. With those, he will be safe in speech and action, because his motives and intentions will be just, and the fire of the militant spirit directed to constructive ends.

Therefore, realising his assets as a disciple in the form of abilities for special work on the way, and confronted with liabilities that must be liquidated before he may enter into the Master life, he stands, in his own place, equipped, ready and resolute, with the settled disposition of the warrior armed against all that threatens to distort, disorganise, confuse and

H

entangle, to strike a blow for the further rending of the veil of illusion that holds his brother back from a fearless advance. For a Master has said : " It is with armed hand, and ready either to conquer or perish, that the modern mystic can hope to achieve his object."

CHAPTER X

THE SANCTITY OF SERVICE

In this chapter I strike the keynote of the disciple's life. It is sanctified service. This keynote has often been struck in these pages because we cannot speak of the full-toned concord of the life of discipleship without the fundamental and ever sounding note of sanctified service. Without that there may be some degree of attainment, some freak of magic, some kind of psychic gymnastic to titillate the nerves or please the eye, but nothing to inspire the soul of man or touch the heart of the Master. There are students who place all their hope upon these illusive shadows that masquerade as spiritual reality, and in time they find themselves more perplexed about the reality of life and far less reliable as a guide than those who make reason alone their deity. But I have the happy recollection that the majority of aspirants I have contacted have had a strong incentive to be of value in the lives of their fellowmen. And I have often been much surprised to find this incentive strong in very young aspirants. From one point of view this is more surprising because of the tone and influence of modern life and circumstances to which these young people are exposed. Some of them are fortunate in this respect in that they have been nurtured in families where the parents have been students of the way, and they have received sympathetic encouragement in their aspirations. Many have had just the reverse of these fortunate conditions ; they are old souls trying to find their past associations on the way in families where they encounter not one spark of understanding or inspiration. But I have a word of encouragement for them : they are perhaps the most fortunate of all, because they have the added force which comes of opposition ; their aspiration and demand are the stronger and more determined, and the door is never long closed to them. They are fortunate because they have taken their novitiate in the past, and nothing in the world of circumstances can prevent their contact with the good influences and associations established in a former cycle, if they are persistent in their search.

Remembering the critical period in which we live, from the evolutionary standpoint, the exceptional opportunities afforded for advancement on the way surpassing anything hitherto known, and the increasing momentum of the thought force of the Masters in human life for its enlightenment and betterment, it is a beautiful thing to find in aspirants young and old this deep and sincere trend towards a life of service. If we needed it, I think this would be one of the strongest arguments in favour of past cycles of evolution of the soul. It certainly argues a considerable measure of growth in the soul, whether in a young or mature personality, that can regard with indifference the many prizes of worldly accomplishment which are more possible perhaps than ever before; that can weigh these with an understanding vision at their true value, and having done so, can say : I desire to serve. I wonder sometimes whether this is partly owing to the growing sensitivity of the human apparatus which can register early and acutely, with a kind of new foresight, and discriminate accurately, without a further repetition of personal experience, the real from the ephemeral. But so it is, and these souls are laying the foundation for the work and illumination of the new age, when " the masks, and mummeries, and triumphs of the world " will pass swiftly and silently away as the shadows at dawn.

I have referred to the assets and liabilities of the disciple. Both are intimately related to the life of service ; and while they appear opposed the one to the other, there is an esoteric connection and a regulative inspiring and retarding interplay between them, all in the direct interest of the disciple's development and of those in Karmic relationship with him. The disciple's assets are, to a large extent, clear and manifest to him, but by no means entirely. He is able to judge the range and value of his work in the world for his fellowmen ; for he has built up a technical equipment through the years far too carefully and laboriously not to be able to use it with effect, or to calculate judiciously the possible reactions to it.

We are thinking of the disciple who is near to the Master and whose work has the imprimatur of the Master upon it. That being so, we expect to see something of the sureness of the Master's own art

operative in whatever field the disciple uses his
technique. Many of his assets will be clear and manifest to him : there are others of which he will not
be fully conscious, because they relate to work and
contacts with Higher Powers on the inner side of
life during meditation and sleep. In these two conditions is the casual life of the disciple's objective
manifestation. This does not require stressing, for
the disciple, in functioning now more as the soul
than the personality, has sympathetic access to the
plane of souls, and his technical ability is derived
therefrom. The source of his technique is in the
superconscious life of the soul universal. He has the
ability to draw upon this superconscious life, but
the channels and senses through which it comes are
not of the objective man but of the indwelling self.
That which is given he uses, but it is largely in meditation and sleep that he must look for the causes of
it ; and these are, in some measure, as hidden to
him as to the veriest tyro on the way until he passes
the portal of initiated consciousness and has actual
cognition of the forces of inspiration and guidance.

Just as these assets are his through the rewarding
Karma of the past, so are the retarding influences of his
liabilities bound up with the same Karma. How many
disciples well on the way, with a developed technique
of service, are retarded from further notable advance
by these liabilities ! They stand near to the Master
and are doing his work, but the illumination they
looked for through the years still awaits them. I have
known such instances, and it has given rise in them
to perplexity and disappointment and a sense of
barrenness and futility in spite of all effort. They

have been very much like Pascal, when the brilliant
work of his hands became a stumbling block and an
offence, when everything even of good seemed to be
passing away from him, when all the accomplish-
ments of the past appeared to count for nothing :
that supreme testing period of blankness and negation before the Christ came to him in fire. But if
the assets in their complete and esoteric nature, are
hidden to the disciple, and only to be deciphered in
the Master's presence, so is it with his liabilities.
Perhaps it is well that the real character of both is
hidden ; for a knowledge of the one might raise a
sense of pride in the disciple ; and a knowledge of
the other would certainly humiliate and discourage
him. We are impatient, but it is well that our eyes
cannot see all they would before the time. " Chafe
not at Karma, nor at nature's changeless laws, but
struggle only with the personal, the transitory, the
evanescent and the perishable," says the scripture.
It is the disciple near to the Master who needs this
admonition more than anyone else on the way. For
he is a high tension individual whose technique
of service is flowering in many directions, and
for this very reason he is impatient of the retarding
influences of Karmic liabilities which in various
circumstances hold him back from the full expression
in perfected service he sees in vision. It is he who
needs to " Remember, thou that fightest for man's
liberation, each failure is success, and each sincere
attempt wins its reward in time. The holy germs
that sprout and grow unseen in the disciple's soul,
their stalks wax strong at each new trial, they bend
like reeds but never break, nor can they e'er be lost.

But when the hour has struck they blossom forth."
And often will he need to remember it ; for it is
not so much now by the strength of his will, tempered like steel as it is, that he will achieve, as by a
tireless patience with life where he stands and a
growing insight into the causes which underlie
his life pattern.

I said there was a regulative inspiring and retarding interplay between the disciple's assets and
liabilities. The justice of being subjected to retarding influences may often be questioned by him ; he
finds it difficult to reconcile this aspect of his life
with the elevating expression of the inspiring aspect
of it, known and acknowledged : but he is as responsible for the one as for the other. And standing on
the right hand of the Master as he may be, he has
to prove his wisdom and insight by acting nobly
and faithfully there, while destined for a certain
term to liquidate the liabilities in intimate relationships of persons and circumstances in many mani-
pulative adjustments in contacts and service.

But should we regard the term inevitably to be
spent in the discharge of Karmic liabilities as retarding, or in any way inimical ? Only from the
personal standpoint, because ambition for attainment has not ceased to assert itself even in the
disciple. Ambition for lesser attainments may have
passed away ; but ambition for things of a higher
nature and forspiritual conquest is not easily extin-
guished. Suppose for instance, and it may be more
than a supposition, the disciple's Karma has brought
him into close contact and co-operation with other
disciples on the way, and together they are working

towards a similar objective. They will be of unequal
development although co-operating esoterically
and objectively in some department of the Master's
work ; and it is necessary for the ultimate end in view
that this unequal development among them should
be in certain respects equalised ; that the objective
cannot be reached until the various Karmic liabilities of all have been adjusted and the soul of the
group freed from the inhibitory bonds which con-
stitute that inequality. That is exactly the position of
many a disciple near to the Master. Not for himself
alone, but for those near him, he has to wait and
serve and carry sympathetically and interpret
understandingly the impinging forces of the Karma
of his co-disciples until there is a balance of power,
wisdom and love which enables them to act in
perfect unison in their esoteric life. That is why
tolerance, compassion and love are so much insisted upon at this stage. The disciple must have no
voice for criticism of the failings of his co-disciples.
For him there must be only the thought of the soul
of love in evolution under its own personal difficulties. However different in personality, in views,
opinions and tastes, whatever the weaknesses,
fugitive errors, incidental failures, under the exigencies of circumstance and the pressure of Karmic
attachments, these must be passed below the threshold of consciousness and only the expression of
true understanding and willing helpfulness appear.
But is not this a condonation of that which merits
rebuke ? What if the Master had rebuke for the
manifold frailties of the disciple ! Nearness to the
Master is not the sign manual of perfected human

nature: far from it. If not the disciple's own Karma, that of the present day world would prohibit it. Why? Because even the disciple, no matter how advanced, cannot live to himself: indeed, he is infinitely more implicated in the world Karma than is the average man. If this is questioned, let a man develop a true sensitivity of discipleship and realise the truth of it. It is this fact, so clear to the Master's vision, which is the guarantee of the latter's loving compassion for the disciple near to him. For all his shortcomings there is no rebuke, but only wise understanding and deeper encouragement in the face of the keen difficulties known so well to him.

Yet there are those who demand of a disciple more than the Master himself demands. These are they who have trodden the way by book and know nothing of its technique. They are so full of theories and their own personality that they would legislate for those incarnations ahead of them. They have the satisfaction of knowing that they increase the burden of the disciple and hinder their own development. The perfected human nature they expect in him they help to make impossible through their own lack of understanding. Their influence is part of the world Karma referred to, and, fortunately, the disciple understands it very well. And if that is one of the penalties of advancement, perchance one of the particular liabilities of a disciple's Karma, the use he makes of it is to probe deeper into the world of causes and emulate the Master in his long range vision and indifference to personal reactions.

Many phases of the working out of the peculiar Karmic liabilities of advanced discipleship could be touched upon, but they all work out to one issue. The disciple's position demands of him one major application in all its difficulties and trials, that of sanctified service. If discipleship is not that it is an experiment only and loses all its stature. It is the one thing that brings him near to the Master, no matter what the world chooses to point as failings and shortcomings, and it is the one justification of him in the eyes of the world unseen. I believe this so deeply that I would say sanctified service covers the multitude of orthodox sins that consign men so self-righteously to hell. This is perhaps a perilous statement, but not from the point of view I choose to make it. We have seen records of the lives of disciples and initiates published years after they have gone to their reward, for the express purpose of attempting to prove them to have been arrant knaves and sinners, while the memory and example of their unremitting labours brighten the path of every rightminded aspirant and ennoble every step of the way. That, too, is a part of the world Karma which their successors have to carry : and they, too, will suffer the same fate, now or hereafter.

We should not expect it to be otherwise, much as we deplore the fact. It has been pointed out that the disciple has a range of values peculiar to his status on the way. They are not self-imposed values : they are imbibed through his intimate contact with the Master consciousness and become the laws of all his future action. He will serve after those laws and under the inspiration of their many-sided technique, often in ways and for purposes quite hidden to the general consciousness. The wonder

is, not that he is much misunderstood by the average
aspirant, but that he is rightly comprehended by
those near him. It is here that he is held by those
Karmic liabilities to serve unfalteringly those near
and far off, who strike the note of relationship in
his life from past cycles of activity. It would be hard
travelling, perhaps too hard even for his feet, if
there were not also those far off and near, who have
an instinctive or enlightened understanding and
appreciation of that service. Perhaps that is the
reward I was asked to point out for those who are
called upon to give so much. It is a very sufficient
reward that others share his labours and seek no
other reward for themselves. That is the true meaning of sanctified service, and beneath the surface
of the bustle and selfishness of modern life there is
much of it. It is this undercurrent of real goodness,
rendered potent and increasing in potency, and fed
perennially by all those converging on the way, no
matter to what school of thought they belong, that
lessens the burden of the disciple's individual Karma
and gives him strength in many a crucial hour. For
where there is real goodness of heart there will be
sanctity of service, different in degree, in aspirant and
disciple according to their attainment on the way,
yet ever present, uplifting and ameliorating. In the
words of the Rosicrucian, Bacon : " The parts and
signs of goodness are many. If a man be gracious
and courteous to strangers, it shows he is a citizen
of the world, and that his heart is no island cut off
from other lands, but a continent that joins to them :
if he be compassionate towards the afflictions of
others, it shows that his heart is like the noble tree

that is wounded itself when it gives the balm : if he easily pardons and remits offences, it shows that his mind is planted above injuries, so that he cannot be shot : if he be thankful for small benefits, it shows that he weighs men's minds, and not their trash ; but, above all, if he have St. Paul's perfection, that he would wish to be an anathema from Christ for the salvation of his brethren, it shows much of a divine nature, and a kind of conformity with Christ Himself." There we have the ritual of goodness in epitome. And the disciple who can willingly embrace " anathema from Christ " in the service of others is not only near to the Master, but very like him.

CHAPTER XI

MYSTICAL QUIETUDE

MAINTAINING the position of an independent observer and impartial critic of various aspects of mystical approach of aspirant and disciple on the way, in the hope that the reflections offered may prove suggestive and helpful to either or both, let us consider a particular quality of the disciple, one which is in fact indispensable to him, during that, often lengthy, term when he stands near to the Master with many Karmic liabilities to be liquidated before the presence of the Christ within him becomes a known and living experience. It was said, that not now so much by the assertion of the will, but through a tireless patience with life where he stands and a deeper insight into the causes underlying his life pattern, will he achieve. To manifest continuous and tireless patience in difficult circumstances necessitates, it need scarcely be said, a sound knowledge of ourselves and not a little knowledge of the circumstances : at least I am sure it does of the kind of circumstances a disciple usually has to deal with. And patience finds its best soil in the quiet mind. How little life around us to-day contributes to the quiet mind, we know only too well. It is the sorrowful plaint of most aspirants on the way, and there is good reason for it. Nor is the advanced disciple indifferent to it : he does his work in spite of it, because, through a measure of developed detachment, mystical quietude is a stable quality in his equipment. Even so, it is not easily maintained. The high grade of sensitivity which enables him to answer to all so readily and invites his participation as an appreciative soul in the world experience, threatens at every step that inner tranquillity so much coveted and so necessary for the highest service.

" The peace you shall desire," says the scripture, " is that sacred peace which nothing can disturb, and in which the soul grows as does the holy flower upon the still lagoons." It is a beautiful thought of a delectable condition ; but it is a far cry from the condition of turmoil of the battlefield for which the disciple has to deliberately prepare himself and in which his engagements are many. We do not doubt the reality or the possibility of the ideal condition of unbroken peace and tranquillity which the eastern scriptures so often bring to us : but it is pardonable if we think they speak of one world while we live in another. Pardonable or not, the fact is so. A description of the ideal world is one thing : living in the present one is quite another ; and if the Masters of life ever forgot that when they turn their attention to the western aspirant, it would be one of the greatest tragedies in this story of evolution. It is what the disciple never can forget when looking at the aspirant feeling his troubled way through a psychic atmosphere of chaotic and destructive influences. I feel intensely on this problem, because

I have so often seen aspirants struggling with it.   I
have seen them turn in despair from the way because
the world atmosphere has been too strong for them.
They could not reach a point of quiet in which to
face the issues of the way.   Time there may have
been, time enough for the strong and resolute soul,
but for them the voice of the world has been too
insistent, too inharmonious, breaking in with violent
disruption upon the sensitive and untutored organism, and they have taken the line of least resistance.

The fact that this is so, and it cannot be disputed,
lays a tremendous responsibility upon the more
advanced man. He has forced his way through one
of the hardest periods of evolution; for the past
years have been cruel in disruptive vibratory influences and a veritable challenge to a peaceful mind.
If he has detachment and serenity and is an example
of mystical quietude, let the aspirant not forget they
have been won in the blood of the heart, and no
otherwise. They are not a gift, but a flowering of
faculty gained on the battlefield of life where the warfare has been hottest and the issue sometimes un-
certain. Yet, because the fact is not published
abroad and the disciple moves on the even tenor of
his way, with a calm and unperturbed demeanour
and an apparent indifference to the world at large, he
is apt to be thought unacquainted with the eventu-
alities and vicissitudes of circumstances in their
darker and aggressive forms and sadly lacking in
necessary experience. It is admitted that there are,
and always have been, drawing room disciples of
undoubted erudition in discussing worlds they know
nothing of and past incarnations they would never

have had the backbone to face; and if the aspirant is led to regard these glorified pundits as proficients in discipleship, he may be forgiven his judgment of them. This department of the occult intelligentsia is outside my province. I am thinking of the working disciple down here on the pavement, and the aspirant may well study his art. He stands foursquare on the earth on which he was born, and leaves speculations about other worlds and unknown heavens to the spiritual dilettante who has nothing else to do.

If there is any truth I would drive home to the aspirant, it is that the disciple I treat of is a thoroughly practical individual, with the same human nature and of like passions and infirmities as himself, facing the same fears and oppositions of circumstances as he is, knowing in their full range and strength the difficulties and temptations which burden the whole human family, and who, nevertheless, has made for himself the opportunities of entering into the life of the soul and imposing its higher rhythm and elevating influence upon the common human factor and taken a step forward in evolution. There is no speculation in that, or assumption of wisdom and power he does not really possess. He regards askance occult theory-mongers and smug purveyors of news from heaven and puts their value on a level with talking politicians. Both species thrive upon etherial Utopias which never materialise; and if the aspirant reposes faith in them, and loses it, as he certainly will, he will at least have learned how to discriminate, although he might have learned much more in the time.

I

The real disciple is not caught in this web of illusion. He knows the sound qualities of discipleship at sight. Mystical quietude is one of these qualities. It is born of knowledge and experience of self and circumstance. It is not gained from books, but from deep communion with the heart of life. Have you not noted how those noble souls who have suffered long and deeply under some cross of circumstance, become mellowed in character and temperament, patient and kind in contact and bless others unconsciously by their presence ? We meet with it in those who know nothing of the way, beyond what their own souls impress upon them. There is something in this akin to the mystical quietude of the disciple who stands near to and yet afar off from the Master, with many Karmic obligations to be met and adjusted. He has felt too deeply and knows too much to be other than of a quiet mind. Discipleship means height : it also means depth : where either is lacking discipleship is not. And so it is, that beneath the mystical quietude of the disciple there is a drama of the soul being enacted at this stage which is grander in compass and more engrossing in detail than anything seen or known in the objective life : but it is a silent drama, rising to climaxes of death and birth, in which the soul and the personality are the players and the Master perhaps not merely a spectator. The world outside knows nothing of this : that is why it makes such ludicrous mistakes in its judgment of discipleship. The aspirant does not know very much about it either : that is why he should learn to be quiet and reserve his judgment. He may easily mistake the mystical quietude which arises from a wise detachment and impersonality for a want of interest and sympathy in matters that appear very important to himself; whereas those matters can only be seen clearly and rightly judged in precisely that condition of mind. He overlooks the fact that the disciple has passed that way in the long journey; that he, too, has questioned much and to little purpose, because an illuminating response is not contingent simply upon knowledge but upon the factors of time and readiness in relation to the aspirant's development. The highest knowledge can fail him utterly in conviction and illumination if the mind is not developed to a right perspective to receive it. When the aspirant thoroughly realises that and looks to himself first instead of to others, then he is on the way to that quietness and receptivity of mind which permits the soul to be his teacher. That is a marked characteristic of the disciple: he questions abundantly, but himself, not others. He knows from experience that the soundless voice within is of more value to him than the voices of authority or the dogma of books. The aspirant need not take my word for it: if he will study the technique of genius he will need no better teacher. Genius knows the value of culture, possesses it and uses it; but it passes beyond that to profound meditation upon the revelation of the soul in silence. Lesser voices are an impertinence to it, but only because it is secure and confident on the height of its own peculiar evolution. There is so much in genius which is akin to the creative disciple that I have often spoken of it as unconscious discipleship.

There is but the difference that genius is mainly intent upon creation in art or science, while the disciple is bent upon the conscious manipulation of personal and higher forces for evolutionary and spiritual purposes. And for this end there must be orderly and systematic development of the whole man to hold and direct the awakening fire of the soul in its descent and inspiration in his chosen work.

At the crucial stage where the disciple stands at the bar of Karma very near to the Master yet without the portal and still feeling his way under the guidance of the soul, mystical quietude must be his in full measure. " Be sure of foot, O candidate. In patience' essence bathe thy soul ; for now thou dost approach the portal of that name, the gate of fortitude and patience." Tireless patience with the circumstances of life under the judgment of culminating Karma finds its true soil in the quiet mind. The aspirant may think that mystical quietude is not so extraordinary an acquisition as it appears to be. He has the text books on concentration and meditation well digested : it is merely a matter of sitting still and keeping the nose under observation, and the world passes away. There is a difference between mystical quietude and mental vacuity, There is indeed a great difference between reposeful interludes at the beginning of the way, when the Karma of past cycles touches the aspirant but lightly on the shoulder, and the ability to demonstrate spiritual peace amid the powerfully developed and highly active forces of the mature constitution of the disciple at the altitude of the way. The forcing methods of innumerable occult books and courses make it necessary to exercise discrimination. They are accessible to all alike, to the most illiterate aspirant as to the most cultured. And what is the result of these methods in either case, where there is no prepared ground for mystical training, perhaps not even a desire for it, but only an ambitious curiosity for a short cut development of a yogic nature to bring thought and emotion to a standstill in order to demonstrate the supremacy of will in a reversal of normal functions? A result of enforced and mechanical quiescence which has no background of higher knowledge or soul contact to inform it, a condition of self-hypnosis far less productive than the condition of natural sleep.

The quietude of the disciple is a quality of high mystical art. Concentration there must be, stillness of the objective mind, meditation profound, and comprehensive knowledge of the soul emerging into and inspiring the personal life, but all this lies behind in the years of hard probation. There is no short cut to the temple of the soul. An inexperienced aspirant is not to blame in believing there is. He puts his faith in the word of plausible writers who hash and rehash the instruction of yoga and promise the illumination and peace of master minds through physical and mental jugglery. But the inevitable disillusionment comes, and with a chastened mind he realises there is such an entity within man as the resident soul, pregnant with the burden of Karmic relationships and responsibilities from the past which has to be met and unveiled and understood and lived before he can hope to near the goal. When he realises that and has built the strength to deal with it, then he will know, as a disciple, the importance and value of mystical quietude.

The last stages of a race or contest are the crucial ones. So it is with the disciple who stands before the portal. Fortitude and patience are written on it. He has crossed the battlefield and proved his strength. He has fought well and made a path that others might follow, and the peace of the Master falls upon him. The invisible mantle of mystical quietude is the armour conferred upon the tried warrior who has lost much in a long struggle that others might win. The sword in his hand is keen and bright; it is the sword of tempered experience, which he will yet use with wisdom and skill against the offending hosts who would rob the aspirant of his right to advance and his eternal reward. For he is a warrior still; and no warrior surrenders his weapons of advance. And while he is still without the portal he stands upon treacherous ground. He needs more vigilance now than ever before. What, is not the Master's influence sufficient for protection ? Not without his own co-operation. However near to the Master, the disciple has his own life to live, and that life is strongly bound and obligated to other lives on the objective and inner planes of experience. His chief lesson now is to understand, with a quiet mind, the meaning of those other lives that stand near and related to him, in work and circumstance, in helpfulness and opposition, in love and hate. It is not now the keen will that cuts its way to the goal, but the manipulation and balancing of human and psychic forces operating through entities of Karma which stand out as clearly to the vision as that entity of Karma which his own soul faces with steady equilibrium and purpose. Figuratively speaking, it is as if the disciple stood at the centre of a circle, with radiations of Karmic connection with others at different stations at the circumference. As time passes, some of those radiations become attenuated and ultimately vanish, the claims of those to whom they attached having been met and liquidated. Conversely, other radiations will increase in tensity and strength and those to whom they attach will be drawn through sympathetic understanding and like stature steadily to the centre and take their place beside him. But a fact so simply stated may require years to work out ; and that is the conscious task the disciple sets himself. Patience, indeed, and ever more patience, until all is reconciled and harmony reigns from centre to circumference of the disciple's field of influence and contact. Nothing can be hurriedly done for his own liberation. In the east, the one aim is liberation, renunciation of circumstances and personalities, almost an abjuration of existence itself, that the soul may pass into absolute, untrammelled and ever lasting freedom. It is not for us to criticise an end which is eminently desirable, although the means are utterly foreign to western ideals. The disciple on the way in the west considers it a dishonourable thing to renounce circumstances to which he knows he is Karmically bound, and an unpardonable sin to repudiate the intimate relationships of personalities to which he knows that for the love of Christ he must remain true. I do not think there is a single earnest aspirant who doubts the truth of this in his heart, no matter how difficult it may be to live. He must not mind the difficulty, but accept it. He will never realise the mystical quietude of discipleship until he does. It is fortitude in circumstances that sear his soul, and patience in accepting all they entail in life, that will unfold in him the true resignation of spiritual peace. So will his life become aligned with the Master's purpose in evolution, and carry that far-seeing wisdom and healing so fruitful in service.

The flower of mystical quietude grows in silence during the storm of the ascent on the way; and before the portal " the whole personality of the man is dissolved and melted " and becomes " a subject for grave experiment and experience." But this is only possible when the disciple stands within the circle, isolated in peace, with all the radiated stations at the circumference held in keenest circumspection and upon which the love of the soul throws its revealing light and extends its willing service.

CHAPTER XII

THE MYSTICAL CHALLENGE

I HAVE briefly sketched, from a particular point of
view, the way of mystical ascent. No more was
attempted. Nor were specific forms of concentration
and meditation offered, since there is a prolific literature available which gives them. The aim has rather
been to hint at definite inner changes which must
ensue under mystical training, and a right appraisal
of reactions in the life and in circumstances which
occur under such training. It is one thing to set
forth a series of concentrative and meditative forms
of procedure, but quite another to follow and
sympathetically interpret, without bias, the manifold
intimate and difficult reactive experiences in heart,
mind and soul which accompany a dedicated effort
to tread the way. If the student says he has been
quite unaware of any particular experiences of this
nature, that he has followed the way for years and
experienced nothing of stress or difficulty in life or
circumstance, then I affirm that he knows nothing
of practical mysticism. If Christ truly pointed the
way of the mystic, there is not a shadow of a doubt
as to what the treading of that way entails. The
same difficulties, the same trials, the same cross,

figuratively speaking, await every son of man who offers himself for the great adventure.

But the full burden of the way is the privilege of very few, for the simple reason that the aspirants are many, the disciples few. Nor do I hesitate to say that the majority of aspirants at the present time are totally incapable of bearing the full burden of the way. A desire for unusual knowledge, the reading of mystical literature, affiliation with mystical societies, are preliminaries necessary and helpful; but not until there is a spontaneous readiness in the whole man to become transmuted in thought, speech and action by converting all these helps into living steps of interior evolution, can a student consider himself really embarked on the way. Moreover, if there is not a predisposition towards it which is very pronounced in the constitution, the plain truth is, that while he certainly can become an aspirant now, the present cycle of life will be mainly taken up with the work of preparation. Emerson said that the tone of seeking was one, and the tone of having another. The unprejudiced aspirant will feel the truth of that before he has gone far on the way. He will be wise to accept what his intuition tells him about his present possibilities and not attempt to overreach himself. No good will come of it. We hear a good deal of the possibility of attaining to Masterhood in one brief cycle of life. I have yet to meet one who has shown such exceptional promise. Types of mastery are possible in one or another direction; but these are only steps on the way to Christhood, and it will demand the best of our present grade manhood to take even those steps. I dissent absolutely from opinions to the contrary, because I have seen nothing to confirm them. I have no wish to discourage the aspirant, but I will not suggest as an easy attainment a goal which is the hardest a man can set himself in this life. If we could live to ourselves in an environment of peace and harmony, with no worldly responsibilities resting upon us, no Karmic ties with other personalities demanding attention and careful adjustment, and could devote ourselves to uninterrupted study and meditation and to the placid enjoyment of natural beauty and artistic communion, much no doubt might be accomplished in a few years in entering into a high contemplative state and unfolding the gifts and graces of mystical faculties. Even so, I do not know that it would be the most desirable goal for the western aspirant. I know it is an impossible one in his particular environment. He finds himself in conditions directly antagonistic to isolated and peaceful mystical attainment. He has to work with his hands and forge ahead with his brain to live, and take such steps as he can to unfold the life of the soul amid the clamour and call of the arrogant world. Perhaps he is the better for it and of far more value to the world, even at considerable loss to himself. We do not expect perfect types in our environment. Nor would they survive in it for long. The best we can hope for, perhaps the highest we can expect to see in these days, is the militant disciple who has weathered the storm and gives a few hints of the perils of the passage to those who are ready to take it themselves.

The most important quality to be made permanent

in the disciple's equipment, after the meditative
and contemplative contact has been fully established, is that of spiritual militancy. This may
be questioned, but I cannot retract. I would re-
emphasise it, and from another aspect. We have
heard the word of peace spoken, with all the varia-
tions of human rhetoric, when there is no peace.
On the contrary, we live virtually in a time of war.
The world atmosphere in which we live is a militant
one. We may close our eyes to it in our prayers and
meditations, but we can no more shut out the world
atmosphere of militancy than we can cease to breathe.
And if our Karma is bound up with the world
Karma, we share in it and have a responsibility in
it. But this surely does not mean that the disciple
must share in the militant tendencies of the world ?
No, not necessarily; but on his own level of life
and in his own sphere of action and service, he must
have aggressive and dominant faculties of a similar
nature if he is to leave any mark of the way he has
gone for those who would achieve now and those
who hope to achieve in the future. He has a world
atmosphere to deal with which is evilly aggressive,
domineering and threatening in its psychic potencies,
and it is impossible to escape its influence; which
means that men are swayed in thought and action
by those potencies far more than they realise. An
impartial observer said : " You talk of the brother-
hood of man : look around you ! " a pertinent
remark and true, although we on the way prefer to
close our eyes and live in an illusion. That remark
is typical of the attitude of the world which the disciple faces to-day. And I ask, what chance has he to

do anything for it, or be of inspiration to anyone
in it, if he is a sentimentally religious and puling
humbug and is afraid to speak the word of power
born in his own knowing soul, even though he
runs counter to the opinions of men, the sterile
church, and all the other blatant authorities, high
and low, who raise their voice against it? There is
always room for a man of force, said Emerson. The
world knows that very well and has found and used
such men. Where is the militant mystic to confront
them?

Indeed, it is a troubling thought that, for all the
widespread interest in and following of the mystic
way in many lands, all eyes and ears are intent upon
the brutish personalities of blood-minded dictators,
and there is not a single inspired apostle combining
in himself the master qualities of Christ and man,
with a message of such compelling force as to seize
upon and compel public opinion. It is humiliating
to poor humanity that, with all its aspiration, blind
or enlightened, towards the divine, there has not
been vouchsafed to it one man of superhuman
character and personality and dynamic forcefulness
to stand forth and arrest the action of insolent
tyrants who, with Machiavellian astuteness, trample
upon the soul and honour of men. You will tell me,
speaking from the chair of academic occultism, that
it is the inevitable and lawful outworking of racial
cleavages and crisis. If I agree, what is that to poor,
suffering humanity who knows nothing of it, and
if it did, would not ease one jot its burden? It is a
thought that must exercise every right-minded
aspirant on the way, whatever his persuasion and

however great his knowledge. The rapine of humanity is before his eyes. He may shut them, but it is still there. And humanity waits for a saviour in human form, but he does not appear.

This is the note on which I close this book. A different note might do more honour to the mystic, but not to the common heart of humanity in which the mystic must live. Yet we on the way, even in our helplessness, may do something. We can combine our thought forces into an intense and militant and living potency against those who commit foul rapine in high places and defraud the sons of men of their birthright, and resolve, in the words of that illustrous son of freedom, to " bring their devilish machinations to naught."

Printed in the United States
1367400001B/192

9 780766 104679